GROWING UP

with

GOD

Using stories to explore a child's faith & life

NANCY COCKS

WILD GOOSE PUBLICATIONS
www.ionabooks.com

Copyright © 2003 Novalis Publishing, St Paul University, Ottawa, Canada

First published 2003 by Novalis Publishing, Canada

UK and Europe edition published 2003 by Wild Goose Publications
Fourth Floor, Savoy House, 140 Sauchiehall Street, Glasgow G2 3DH, UK
web: www.ionabooks.com

Wild Goose Publications is the publishing division of the Iona Community.
Scottish Charity No. SCO03794. Limited Company Reg. No. SCO96243.

ISBN 1 901557 74 X

Cover design © Wild Goose Publications
Interior layout: Caroline Gagnon
Interior images: S. McNamara (p146), Anne Côté (p176), EyeWire (p208)

A catalogue record for this book is available from the British Library.

Printed and bound by Bell & Bain, Thornliebank, Glasgow, UK.

GROWING UP

with

GOD

In memory of my father,
whose love for telling stories
inspired my love of stories

Acknowledgments

This book is the fruit of several years of research and storytelling with families and church leaders who live in many different places. Protecting the identities of people whose insights are quoted in the book means that I cannot acknowledge by name all those who have earned my thanks. Nevertheless I am deeply grateful to my Canadian colleagues in ministry who helped me contact families in their congregations and to the children and parents across the country who participated in my research. Without their co-operation, enthusiasm and hospitality, I could not have completed this project. I owe The Iona Community in Scotland my appreciation for the opportunity to spend a summer working with children on the Isle of Iona, and colleagues John L. Bell, Norman Shanks and Sandra Fox for helping to arrange my visit there.

I also want to thank The Vancouver School of Theology (VST) and The Ewart Endowment for Theological Education for their financial support and encouragement during the sabbatical terms in which I conducted the research and completed the manuscript for *Growing up with God*. Vancouver School of Theology, where I taught for nearly ten years, demonstrated its commitment to scholarship for the church and its vision for the place of children in Christian community through its recognition of my research. I remain deeply grateful to my colleagues there. I wish to thank my two research assistants, Janice Love and Sharon Salomons, now graduates of VST, for their invaluable insights as we worked together on both the interviews and the completion of the manuscript.

I owe thanks to several friends who read the various drafts of this book and made extremely helpful suggestions to improve it: Sallie McFague, Eric Muirhead, Jean Morris, Harry Maier and Jane Kilthei. Finally, I want to acknowledge the ongoing support and co-operation of Novalis. More than ten years ago, staff at Novalis responded with enthusiasm to a few stories about Fergie the Frog that I submitted more or less on a whim. Kevin Burns, who arrived much later on the scene, picked up those stories and this manuscript with an instinctive appreciation for my approach to storytelling. Anne Louise Mahoney has worked on the details of this text and others with wisdom and good humour. Suzanne Nussey copyedited the text. I want to thank Kevin for his encouragement at a crucial time in the unfolding of my research and Anne Louise for her ability to match clarity with creativity. They have shown remarkable flexibility in all this as I made my transition from Vancouver to Scotland, working across time zones without waking me up too early in the morning as deadlines drew near.

Nancy L. Cocks
Isle of Iona
October 2002

Contents

Introduction

The Heart of the Matter

Beth stopped to shake my hand as she left the worship service one Sunday morning. "I got a new kitten this week," she announced. Then she held up her index finger for my inspection. "On Tuesday the cat scratched me. See?" I looked. A faint scratch was visible. Beth continued, "I prayed that God would take the cat scratch away. Why is it still there?" A crisis of faith at age five. Beth also took insulin by injection every day for diabetes. As her minister, I suddenly began to wonder how often she prayed that God would take away her needles.

On her way home from school, Kate knocked on the door of the manse where I lived. She had something on her mind. We sat on the front step to talk. "What would you do if you were a little girl and there was another bigger girl who was saying mean things about you at school? To the teachers and everybody." A little sister myself, I recognized in her question the schoolyard rivalry between Kate and her older sister. I had heard their sibling squabbles at church functions. It wasn't hard to imagine how sisters, aged seven and nine, might continue to provoke each other on the playground.

Penny chatted to me about her plans for Christmas one evening when I was visiting her family's home during Advent. We had been talking about Christmas trees, comparing the appeal of a real tree to the artificial one the family wanted to replace. Penny stared into the flame of an Advent candle for a minute and then looked at me. "If

Jesus came to bring us life," she wondered, "why do we kill Christmas trees to remember his birth?" An eight-year-old environmentalist, "stumped" by the logic of a throwaway culture.

Each of these episodes has a serious question at its heart; these questions I've pondered during my years as a minister and teacher. The questions Beth, Kate and Penny asked continue to puzzle other young minds. The same questions puzzle adults who want to respond in ways that help a child grow in faith. As the chapters of this book unfold, I will return to each of these questions, one by one, to explore the matter on each child's heart. I've received many such questions from children with whom I've worked over the years. These questions have provoked me to reflect on how church communities help children "grow up with God." This book offers the fruit of my reflection. This is a book for adults who are eager to encourage children around them to know and trust God. It is for parents and grandparents, teachers and leaders, ministers and priests, for any adult who cares about the spiritual lives of children. Together we will explore a way in which storytelling can help adults and children talk about things that matter deeply to us – and to God, who loves us.

Welcoming a Child

In the Gospel of Mark, Jesus is recorded as saying, "Whoever welcomes one such child in my name welcomes me, and whoever welcomes me welcomes not me but the one who sent me" (Mark 9.37). Jesus' attention to children in his community frames my experience as a child in a local church. I grew up as part of a Presbyterian congregation in Canada during the 1960s. The church had a well-organized "Sunday School" in those days. My parents, who were volunteer teachers, took me each week. At church I met many adults who knew my name and gave me interesting things to do. I sang in the Junior Choir. I performed in pageants. Eventually I read Scripture lessons during worship. I found the community of my local church a welcoming place.

Once I reached university, I moved to the fringes of a new congregation, but there I experienced God's call to ministry. Undoubtedly, my early experience in Christian community opened me to that possibility. It also shaped my approach as a leader in the church. I spent many summers working with children at church camp and in vacation activity programs. When I was ordained as a Presbyterian minister, I set out to offer to other children the kind of welcome I had received in church as a child. I wanted children to know that I was *their* minister, interested in their lives and their concerns, not just those of their parents. In my first parish, it was the custom to have a "children's time" during the weekly worship service. For a few minutes the children gathered at the front of the church to talk about something with the minister. But what should we talk about? I wondered. Good material was hard to find. Many stories moralized, reducing the Good News of God's amazing grace to good behaviour. Other resources relied on object lessons, using ideas too complex for small children. Well do I remember their puzzled looks one Sunday when I tried to compare God's transforming love to a beautiful recycled tin can! Eventually I recalled the childhood afternoons I spent imagining stories with my sister. We gave every toy in the house its own dramatic role. We created a world full of adventures. And so I began to make up stories again to use in "children's time," stories that form the heart of this book.

This story collection grew as I prepared to preach each Sunday. Stories sprouted in my imagination as I considered how some theme from the Scripture readings for the week touched the lives of children. My stories always tapped some childhood memories. Not only did I recall moments in my own life, but I also remembered what I'd observed among children around me. I tried to portray situations that most people could recognize from their growing years, no matter what their current age. I began to tell these little stories in worship, pausing after the story to wonder aloud how God helps us face the situation we'd just imagined. Then I led a short prayer offering our feelings about that situation to God. I believe that these stories, linking familiar childhood episodes with God's concern for us, encouraged children to tell me their stories and ask their important questions about cat scratches and big sisters and caring for God's earth.

Since my days serving as a parish minister, my life continues to be filled with stories. I have taught in a theological college, preparing students for ministries of pastoral care. There we spent a lot of time learning to listen to people tell important stories that reflected both their faith in God and their questions about life. As a pastor and as a professor, I began to sense that church leaders have not directed enough of our listening skills to children. We have spent hours recruiting teachers, selecting curriculum materials and running creative programs for children of different ages. Generations of children have grown up in those programs, but then many – too many – have left the church, gradually drifting away or storming off in defiance. Sometimes such folk have made their way back to church as adults, perhaps with their own children in tow. Often these people have a story from their childhood that needs telling. A question from their youth still lingers in their souls. Somehow our best organizing efforts on behalf of children have missed an essential component. Children have stories to tell that have never been told. Children have questions to ask that have never been explored.

"Ask, and it will be given you" (Matthew 7.7). These challenging words of Jesus echo in my mind whenever a child asks me a question with faithful implications. How can my response invite that child to continue to search for faith and understanding? How do I communicate to every child that her story is welcome and that his question is worthy to be explored, even if there is no easy answer? For me, this is the heart of the matter. How can a new generation of church leaders and parents of faith help a new generation of children to grow up loving God?

Storytelling is vital in facing this challenge. Storytelling communicates the subjects of our concern while passing along the wisdom of one generation to another. Storytelling also builds a special relationship between tellers and listeners in which our hearts are opened to

each other. The stories in this collection encourage children to tell trusted adults the stories that matter to them. We can help children grow up trusting God to be at the centre of their lives
— by telling children stories that speak of their genuine concerns,
— by listening to the stories that children long to tell, and
— by exploring together the questions that children raise – about God, about life and about how to live faithfully in God's world.

The Story Project

In order to listen to the stories and concerns of a new generation of children, I invited a number of families, parishes and local church groups for children to join *The Story Project*. Volunteers came from several different Christian traditions and lived in different regions of Canada. They used a collection of stories I had written, along with short reflections, questions and prayers, to see if and how the interests of children might surface in conversations stimulated by storytelling. Participants offered both written comments and face-to-face interviews describing their experience. Some of the stories I've written are also used by Roman Catholic educators in their classrooms; I have included some insights children shared in that setting. I also used these stories with children from Britain during a summer program on the Isle of Iona. There, too, I heard the concerns of children from different cultural and Christian backgrounds. This book is the result.

The Story Project opened my eyes to a variety of ways in which storytelling affects the budding spiritual life of young children. I hope you will find the conversations reported in these pages thought-provoking. Children aged four to twelve have offered their candid comments about who God is and how God touches their lives. Adults who told stories report on their conversations with children and the questions those conversations provoked. The challenges families and parishes faced when they listened to children wonder aloud about God are also examined. These volunteers speak in their own words in Part I of this book. Their names, and a few details particular to local situations, have been changed to protect identities. I have sorted the contents and comments from our conversations into four chapters that will help you do the following:

— understand this storytelling model and how it unfolds,
— examine the themes of Christian faith at work in the stories and reflections,
— listen to children praying in response to stories, and
— consider ways to use this material at home, in children's programs and in worship.

Part II presents twenty-five stories selected from those tested by *The Story Project* volunteers. Part III offers a comprehensive index to help you find stories on various themes, as well as some suggestions on how to follow up puzzling questions that arise in conversation about the stories. You will quickly see that children are curious about God and God's ways. Given a chance, they can ask very provocative questions!

Before we listen in on *Story Project* conversations, let me set out the convictions that shaped my research goals and focus my findings. I recognize children as people of faith in their own right. God engages them moment by moment and does not wait for children to attain a certain age before inspiring their faith. By "faith" I mean *trust in God*. For me, *God* names the holy and mysterious One who is our *Source* of Life, the *Face* of love and mercy, the *Spirit* of truth and courage. Each of these phrases points to one person in the Trinity, for I am a Christian who has come to know God through the stories and songs of Trinitarian tradition. Yet the roots of my faith draw on a wellspring of trust in God that goes deeper than what I can say about God in words. What I think about God, or at least how I express my thinking, has changed over the years. My trust in God has remained constant. When I talk about God with children, I listen for what they think at the moment. I know that many of their ideas and words will change as they grow. But I hope that children are learning to tap God's wellspring of trust when they hear stories speak the truth of their lives – a truth that God honours as they grow.

The Story Project grew out of this hope. This material does not advocate the teaching of any particular Church or creed, although my own experience of God cannot help but express itself. Shaped by Presbyterian tradition, I am an ecumenical Christian. I have been privileged to work with people from many different churches in many different countries. My own faith has been inspired by stories of God's justice and mercy told by friends and colleagues around the world. Sharing our stories is the heartbeat of the body of Christ. When we tell our stories to one another, we are speaking in the presence of God. What role does such conversation play in a child's sense of place in God's world? The goal of *The Story Project* is really to hear each other speak, heart to heart, of what matters to us – and to the God who loves us.

In this model, sharing stories leads to praying the stories that matter to us. *The Story Project* is not only interested in the *faith* of children. This book also proposes a way for children to begin a *spiritual life*. In my view, our spiritual life involves some essential features:

— thinking about God and our place in God's world,
— opening ourselves to God in prayer,
— seeking and responding to God in worship, and
— offering to God and to each other action that is kind and just, wherever we find ourselves.

As the prophet Micah put it, "What does the Lord require of you but to do justice, and to love kindness, and to walk humbly with your God?" (Micah 6.8). To do this, we begin where we are, whatever our age, on the ordinary days of our lives. As Jesus' disciples, we follow each other's footsteps. Our path won't be easy. We won't get it right all the time. But this is the path where God's good gifts will be found. A healthy spiritual life is formed as wise people of God teach those who are learning how to recognize God in our lives. One generation teaches another, not only by its acts of faithfulness great and small, but also through humbling failures confessed to God and to one another. So whether our faith is strong or shaky, whether our prayers are whispered or proclaimed, we all have stories to share. Each one of us can encourage the other to take the next step in seeking God.

Sometimes it seems a bit overwhelming to begin a conversation about God and what matters deeply to us. Many adults were not encouraged as children to talk about faith in God or the questions faith inspires. Those who discovered God in their lives as adults may find it a challenge to speak to children about God in ways that make sense to a child. Depending on your experience, you may wonder what you'd say to the questions Beth or Kate or Penny raised in the opening paragraphs of this introduction. This book is shaped to help you consider such questions and concerns from a child's point of view and explore ways to respond.

Whatever faith you hold, whatever kind of spiritual life you seek (or avoid!), you will find a partner in these pages. *Story Project* volunteers came from a wide variety of backgrounds. Some were long-time members of a particular Christian tradition; others were quite new to church. A few had training in theological school. Others had little instruction of any sort in Christian teaching. With curiosity and courage they plunged into the project because they all enjoyed stories – and because they all care about children. If you care about children, you have something to share with a child. Wherever you have been on life's journey thus far, you have a story to tell.

"What story should I tell?" you may ask. In *Story Project* workshops, participants sometimes wonder if it isn't more important to tell Bible stories to young children. This is an important concern, especially in this generation. I grew up hearing Bible stories every day – in school, at bedtime, at church, even on television. Certainly in public settings today, Bible stories are no longer common. Many children *and* many adults do not know many Bible stories, even though Bible stories are part of the "family album" of the Church. If we want to root children in Christian faith, they need to learn Bible stories as part of their heritage. My stories were never intended to replace Bible stories or other kinds of religious instruction in a child's life and learning. To introduce children to Bible stories, check for resources published through your church. Different churches read the Bible in somewhat different ways. They teach Bible stories with different emphases. Likely you will discover helpful resources to explore the Bible in your local parish or congregation. Bible stories for children are offered now in many formats. You can find good collections of Bible stories, rewritten to suit different age groups, in libraries near you. There are videos and CD-ROMs available, too, that tell Bible stories in appealing ways.

It was not my goal in *The Story Project* to explore the place of Bible stories in family life, however. *Story Project* material develops themes from Christian faith rooted in and inspired by biblical interpretation. This approach adds an important dimension to the ways we teach Bible stories and the meaning of Christian faith. The stories in Part II of this book help a child relate the significance of God's "Story" to everyday situations. Sharing these stories creates opportunities for adults and children to pursue important questions about God and God's world, to think and talk about the ambiguities of life, to wonder about what might happen if…. In conversation with children, you will likely recall stories of your own to tell. When we explore stories of any sort drawing on this model, children develop their own ability to reflect on things that happen in light of their trust in God.

The conversations recorded in these pages offer delightful moments when we hear the wisdom of children speaking plainly about what matters to them. They name what they see because they have not yet learned the caution adults often feel about expressing themselves. So we smile at the way children put things. We nod when, in youthful candour, a child touches a really important question in a simple and direct way. We may even laugh out loud when a child proposes an idea that is either astonishing in its insight or amusing in its point of view. The concerns children hold deeply, the situations that worry them, the prayers they pray – all these will move us. Whether we smile or frown at a child's comment, it is important to remember that, without guidance, a child's insight cannot always follow its own concern through to a helpful conclusion. The wisdom of children in these pages invites trusted adults to walk with them further, to learn together how to live wisely in God's world.

There is one surprising discovery from *The Story Project* to which I should alert adults who dip into these stories: your heart will not escape untouched.

Parents and group leaders using these stories discovered that their own life situations and their faith in God have been called up for fresh reflection. Those who teach children discovered that they, too, have questions about God that need pursuing. Even grown-ups find that more growing with God awaits them. Sometimes children become our fearless guides, exploring terrain as yet unknown in their experience – which turns out to be tender turf in ours! If we are honest with ourselves, we will find that what matters to children often matters deeply to adults as well. The challenge is to help children explore issues in ways appropriate for their age and experience while seeking for ourselves the mature counsel and fresh understanding that can heal an old wound or shed new insight on a lingering puzzle. Welcoming a child's earnest questions about God invites us to welcome the probing action of the Holy Spirit in our lives, too.

This is a book for travelling companions on a journey of faith. Whatever age we are, we can "grow up" in God. Our trust in God's presence and mercy can deepen. Our wonder and praise can be more fully steeped in God's mystery and majesty. We can widen the horizons of our thinking about God's desire for the world. Eric, a thoughtful eight-year-old boy, considered a question of mine: How would you tell someone about God? His six-year-old brother had already responded quickly with picture words: "God is very big. And has a moustache." Somewhat more tentatively, Eric offered these words: "God is everywhere." He paused and then continued. "But we all have a little piece of God in our hearts."

That's the heart of the matter. How can faithful people in every generation help each other discover and trust the "little piece of God," the very presence of God with us in our lives day by day? As Jesus said to those who came seeking him, "Come and see" (John 1.39).

Part I

Exploring a Child's Faith and Life Through Stories

Chapter 1

Listening by Heart

I want to tell you a story:

One Sunday morning in December I visited a church I'd never attended before. The place was a hive of activity. Along with the special event that drew me to the service, there were several pre-Christmas projects beginning – a food drive for the hungry, pageant practice, plans for a Christmas craft sale. As I found a seat, I noticed an energetic hum around me – whispered greetings, hurried consultations, excited invitations. Even as the opening hymn began, the buzz continued while latecomers squeezed in, struggling out of jacket sleeves, hunting for hymn books. The minister's greeting and opening prayer did not still the murmuring. When the children were invited forward for "Children's Time," thundering feet responded. At least 60 young children slipped out of their seats and swarmed down the aisles. As they gathered on the chancel steps, tiny shrieks of greeting burst forth. Amid the wiggles and whispers, the minister dared to speak:

"I want to tell you a story…"

Immediately, a hush fell over the sanctuary. Every child turned to look at the minister, who was now seated in their midst. Adults settled instantly, listening in expectation. I could feel anticipation hovering. The church sanctuary was transformed, in the blink of an eye, with those magical words, "I want to tell you a story."

There is a wonder in storytelling that can still the bustle of our lives for a while. Stories have taken centre stage again in this generation to spin their power in ways old and new. Storytellers gather in workshops and festivals to refine their skills and display their art. Audiences flock to hear novelists read their work aloud. Short stories travel the radio waves. Television and movies weave tales that draw us in again and again. We *will* sit still for a good story. Storytellers have known this for thousands of years.

The power in storytelling is making an impact in an astonishing number of professions, too. From counselling to mathematics, storytelling finds a place in problem solving these days. Biblical scholars and theologians study the influence of narrative to form, inform and reform God's people. In *The Call of Stories*, respected Harvard psychiatrist Robert Coles describes how he began to use stories to teach medical students to listen to their patients.[1] One person's story calls to another, he learned, as his students began to explore their personal responses to stories they had read. The stories awakened in them a fuller appreciation for each unique life, whether fictional character or flesh-and-blood patient. Coles' approach has influenced education in other disciplines that seek to examine the fabric of human life as part of professional development. Noted author Martha Nussbaum, a professor of law and ethics, relies on fiction to broaden classroom discussions of contentious public policy issues. She discovered that novels give human faces to the implications and consequences of policy.[2] Stories enrich our understanding of what human lives hold in common and why each life has a distinct voice that deserves to be heard.

The Story Project grew out of my trust that God's hopes for the world are somehow involved in this human fascination with stories and the power of stories to transform the way we see God's world. Every story we hear engages our imaginations – whether it's a Bible story, a news clip, a family memory, or a tale from the library shelf. We become a part of that story's world for a while, feeling our way through the action, getting to know the characters. As we explore a story's world,

Just as each tradition has unique stories, so too has each family. Family stories have spiritual power in the lives of children. I listened with my heart when my mother talked resentfully about being sent to church alone. I came to value the fact that my family went to church together. I was astonished by my father's account of being crushed under a falling crate of farm machinery and intrigued by his tales of life in hospital. Stories of good times and hard times helped me trust God and listen for God in my own heart.

Learning stories from so many traditions has never shaken my faith in the God revealed in the stories of Abraham and Sarah, Mary and Joseph and Jesus. Listening to so many stories for so many years has taught me to love and respect stories. At church and at school, from family memory and bedtime story, I learned that stories work in different ways. A story often presents its truth and wisdom through imagination, humour, even exaggeration. The world of stories prepared me for the world around me, to see it and question it and imagine its possibilities. A child's gift of imagination, I believe, is a gift of God, a gift that draws on God's love and mercy, a gift that builds on God's promise of justice and peace. Imagination is a gift nurtured by stories.

Once upon a Time

"Once upon a time...." Generations of listeners recognize these words as an invitation into a story. These words bring us to the doorstep of the unexpected, where we can meet unusual characters doing things we likely never before imagined. "Once upon a time" invites children beyond the world of their own experience into a time that cannot be measured by school time or sleep time or birthday party time. In this visionary world, animals may speak, children perform daring acts to defeat giants, and rough fairy-tale justice triumphs over wicked kings and queens, trolls and selfish people. Yet, in the world of "once upon a time," children meet aspects of their own lives, too.

Brothers and sisters compete; parents are not perfect; bad things happen to good people; people have to try over and over again to achieve important goals. As a make-believe story unfolds in a child's imagination, that child's life story also begins to unfold. Feelings are remembered; struggles to achieve are once more engaged; unfairness is recognized; disappointment is linked to perseverance. Stories help children interpret their experience. At the same time, stories open up new possibilities for the future.

However, the world of "once upon a time" is not a peaceful place these days. The role of fairy tale and myth in the development of young children is hotly debated. Some proponents argue that fairy tale symbolism plays a significant role in children's psychological health. Other commentators see great danger in the violence or the gender roles portrayed in folk tales; they are concerned that children will absorb inappropriate models for their own lives. Feminist research has had special concern for the impact of traditional fairy tales on girls' self-understanding. A contribution to this debate lies beyond the research goals of *The Story Project*. But fairy tales and the stories in this collection share two important characteristics.

First, the world of "once upon a time" presents truths about human life through fiction. The characters in this story collection share the imaginary power through which animals speak and act in many folk tales. Can children distinguish what is "true" about life and about God, who gives us life, from what is imagined and "merely" part of a make-believe story? Children's responses in *The Story Project* illustrate just how quickly children begin to distinguish between real and pretend. Yet pretend stories help them work on real issues, as you will hear. More intentionally than most folk tales, my stories aim to explore situations that many of today's children will recognize at home, at school, and in the wider world. As one parent in the research project commented, "It's amazing how these little stories helped me to hear what my children are saying about their own beliefs and relationships."

Second, it is important to remember that young children make meaning from stories and symbols differently than adults do. James Fowler has studied how children's thinking and speaking about God develops as they grow. His book *Stages of Faith* offers helpful examples as children of different ages talk about their faith and concerns. He comments that in the elementary school years, children respond to narrative, drama and myth "as ways of finding and giving coherence to experience."[4] However, they often communicate their reflections by telling another story rather than summing up meaning in a theme or concept as adults do. Conversations from *The Story Project* illustrate how children work out the meaning of life and faith very concretely, starting from the child's current point of view. Providing the opportunity to talk about what a story calls up within a child encourages this ability to reflect on the meaning of life. As adults who listen, we have to be prepared to start where the child starts to explore meaning and possibility together.

During *The Story Project*, volunteers used stories in this collection in many different settings – home, class, worship, activity group. Parents and teachers observed that children five and under enjoyed best those stories and characters that portrayed situations the children themselves were facing. Children whose world centres on family and home relate readily to stories that explore the ups and downs of getting along with brothers and sisters. They understand a character who disobeys a rule and has to face some consequences. Once children move into wider circles of relationships, they develop greater interest in stories about friendship, facing new challenges and making choices. The power of stories is at work as children grow, helping them learn to interpret things that happen. When stories recreate settings and situations a child has already experienced, that child can reconsider what actual events and relationships mean. But stories also expand a child's experience. When a story presents a new situation, the story in some way prepares the child to face that reality when or if it arrives.

A parent in *The Story Project* put it this way: "I found that these stories and their questions gave us the chance to talk about some issues and values that don't necessarily come up until there's a problem." For unlike the "happily-ever-after" endings of fairy tales, many of my stories end in the middle of a situation. A character faces a choice. A little brother feels sad or mad or sheepish. A little girl needs to apologize to a friend. A parent and child look at a problem together. At a crucial moment, storyteller and listener step out of the drama. Together, they reflect about how it feels to be in the midst of that episode. They may strategize about what to do. The world of "once upon a time" becomes the world of "next time this happens…" and "when I feel this way, I can…." And then they can explore what it means to be a child of God in that moment. They can consider God's guiding love and how a child of faith can live trusting in that love.

The encouragement we give to children to explore faith in God as part of their life story is vital if they are to grow up trusting God. Yet talking about God often leads to conflict about what we "should" believe and how we "should" live. To avoid conflict about these "shoulds," many of us simply don't discuss what we believe in our heart of hearts. As a parish minister preparing parents for the baptisms of their children, I often sensed parents' reluctance to talk about what they believed – and what they struggled with. Some expressed the desire to let children "make up their own minds" about faith. I think this desire often reflects an early experience of being forced to take on religious life as a given, rather than receiving it as a gift offered freely. Parents who still carry childhood resentment of arbitrary expectations associated with church life sometimes reject any role for the Church to teach children about God and shape their spiritual lives.

Yet, for Christians, faith is not a private matter. Faith is rooted in the stories of hundreds of generations of God's people. Parents do not do their children a favour by saying nothing about what they believe. By telling the stories that have shaped us and what we now believe, we give our children the raw material with which the Spirit of God helps them build their own foundation for a life of faith. We can also talk with them about our own struggles to believe and to live what we believe, for children very soon know this same struggle. Our stories can call to their stories. When we encourage children to tell stories and ask questions, we honour their personal journeys with God. We respect them as believers. Encouragement and respect draw us together in true Christian community.

The model examined in *The Story Project* offers a gentle way to open up conversations on topics that matter deeply to young listeners. Using the reflections, questions and prayers that follow each story, parents and children can find natural ways to talk about God and with God. Thinking about these stories encourages children to trust God as a partner in everyday life, a partner whose love can make a difference in every situation they face. A mother summed it up:

> We learned that talking and reading about our faith as a family needs to be a consistent thing. We started to get a better sense of how each child thinks about people, friends and family as we talked about these stories.

Here is an example of the storytelling model in this collection. It features a story that explores a common childhood experience: feeling afraid in the dark.

Fearless Fergie

featuring Fergie the Frog

Faith theme: *We can't see God. God is always with us.*
Life situation: *Being afraid of the dark*
Feeling: *Fear*

"Fergie, are you afraid of the dark?" asked Roger, Fergie's best friend.

"Who? Me?" said Fergie. "Not me! I'm not afraid of anything!"

"Good!" said Roger. "Then let's explore the hollow log tonight."

Fergie swallowed a gulp. "The haunted hollow log?"

"Yup!" Roger nodded. "You're not afraid, are you?"

"Oh no, not me," Fergie squeaked. "I'll meet you there tonight."

"Right!" said Roger. "At midnight."

While everything else was sound asleep, the two little frogs sneaked through the dark forest. The moon and the stars were the only ones watching.

The haunted log was a huge old tree that had fallen many years ago. It had rotted hollow in the centre, and it was so long, you couldn't see from one end to the other. Rumour had it that the log was haunted by a marsh creature.

"You wait here, Fergie, while I go to the other end of the log," Roger directed. "When I call, we'll both go in at the same time. Then we can meet in the middle."

"You mean, go in – alone? In the dark?" Fergie peered at Roger in the moonlight.

"Sure! You're not chicken, are you?" asked Roger.

"Oh no," said Fergie so calmly that his feet were shaking.

In a minute or two, Roger shouted, "OHH-KAAY!" His voice rang in the empty woods. Fergie thought about going back to bed – he was a little afraid of the dark. But he didn't want to be chicken.

"Roger will be there, too. It will be okay," Fergie thought to himself. So into the hollow log he hopped.

It was very dark. Every time Fergie hopped, he slipped on the wet wood. He went very, very slowly. Once he hopped into a cobweb and it nearly scared him skinny.

"Soon I'll meet Roger and it will be okay," Fergie whispered.

When Fergie figured he was at least halfway along the log, he slid out a foot – and gasped! He touched something smooth and cold and slimy.

"Roger? Is that you?" Fergie asked hopefully.

But no one answered Fergie.

Somewhere else another little voice asked, "Fergie, is that you?" Roger had also felt something cold and wet and slippery. But no one answered Roger.

About thirteen seconds later, two little frogs were hopping like crazy through the forest.

"Roger?"

"Fergie! Whew, am I glad to see you!" Roger was shaking like a leaf.

"You weren't afraid, were you, Roger?" Fergie asked.

"Who me? Oh no. I'm not afraid of the dark," declared Roger.

"Me neither," Fergie agreed.

"Besides, you were there. You just didn't answer me when I poked you, right? I wasn't scared. I mean, it was you I touched – wasn't it?" Fergie asked.

Fergie looked at Roger and Roger looked at Fergie. Then they hopped as fast as fleas back to their beds. And they decided the next time they explored the hollow log, they would go in from the same end at the same time – at noon on a very sunny day!

Reflecting on the story

If we're alone, if it's dark, if we hear sounds that make us imagine scary things, it's good to remember that God is always with us, right there, even in the dark. And when we remember that God is always closer to us than the breath inside us, the dark is never quite as scary.

Talking about the story

- Can you remember a time you felt a little scared in the dark?
- When you feel a little scared, what helps you feel better?

Praying after the story

God of night and day, you made the dark and the light. And you are always there. Whenever we feel afraid, help us remember that you are there. Give us courage like a deep breath and peace like a gentle sigh. Amen.

The Work of Stories

Often when I tell *Fearless Fergie*, there is a moment in the story when I sense that every listener feels a bit of fear. We are in the hollow log, holding our breath. (And so, in the last line of the prayer, I invite children to breathe in – and then out – with me!) Adult listeners often ask afterwards, "What was in the log?" Children never ask me that question. They have already imagined what slimy thing the little frogs touched. For them and for me, their imagined view is what matters. This reminds me that children work with stories differently than adults do.

Psychologist Dan McAdams has produced a very helpful study describing how children of different ages use stories to develop their self-understanding and to test ways of interacting with the world. In his book *The Stories We Live By,* he explores how elementary school children respond to what he calls "story themes."[5] A story theme sums up what characters in a story want and how they pursue their goals through its plot. The most common story themes in Western literature are *power* and *love.* As a story theme, *power* refers to the goals a character pursues and achieves through *action. Love* signifies the importance of forming and maintaining *relationships. Fearless Fergie* demonstrates both these story themes.

— *Power:* Fergie is challenged to act by exploring the haunted hollow log, even though he is at least a little afraid.

— *Love:* He doesn't want to disappoint his friend and risk losing Roger's respect.

Power and love are connected through the story because the characters find it easier to act when they think that a friend is nearby.

The stories in this collection effectively draw children into conversation; their ability to do so grows out of the basic story themes portrayed. Power and love in some way move in all these little adventures. Some stories focus mainly on how we use our power and the consequences of acting in certain ways. Other stories are more concerned with relationships and how we learn to build or repair them. Many stories involve the ways in which our actions and our relationships influence each other. Whatever theme a story suggests, each story explores the feelings and choices children face as their world expands. To embrace God and be embraced by God in the midst of these discoveries is a vital dimension of growing up with God. The power and love of God help us consider how we can respond as children of God when we are caught up in a similar situation. *Fearless Fergie* helps a child cope with fear by trusting that God is close by.

McAdams develops the basic story themes of power and love into the broader concepts of *agency* and *communion.*[6] If we think about the challenges of growing up, the terms *agency* and *communion* help us consider the expanding world of childhood. Born or adopted into a family, a child experiences some sort of communion in a close web of relationships. The child soon begins to act as "agent," testing parents in a variety of ways with charming smiles, first steps and the vehement declaration, NO! As a child encounters daycare, church, school and other interests, the child finds wider communion in relationships with peers, friends, teachers. Before long this larger circle of acquaintances produces relationships in which tension, disappointment and uncertainty mix with encouragement, fun and respect. The child's growth as an agent presents that child with consequences of behaviour which are sometimes unexpected or undesired. The child wonders, Who am I? Who will be with me? What shall I do next? These questions take a lifetime to explore, to be sure. However, in the age group for whom these stories are designed, ages four through nine, children make crucial discoveries and draw important conclusions about themselves and their possibilities for acting and relating to others.

The next part of this section introduces the ways in which different characters in the story collection appeal to children's experiences. I have used McAdam's categories of *agency* and *communion* to suggest when and how different stories may be appropriate for children of different ages. Comments from both children and parents will give you a sense of how children speak about these large themes in their own terms and why these themes are important to them. Sometimes, however, children respond to the central character in a set of stories rather than to a story theme. This introduction will also give you a little flavour of the three major characters who star in my stories. Perhaps one will have particular appeal for your young listeners. All this is intended to help you consider how to begin to use this material. At the end of the book, the stories are also indexed according to the life situations, feelings and faith themes that they explore.

It is worth noting that *The Story Project* families simply picked up the stories and began to share them. There really is no code to predict the issue a child may identify in a story. Nor is there a "right meaning" that explains any story. In this model, the stories intend only to evoke a feeling or a memory in the child's experience and invite reflection or discussion about that experience. One father reflected, "The conversations resulting from these stories were really good for both of us. It made me think deeply about how to answer moral questions rather than simply using the same old responses."

There are other storytelling models for children that attach a moral to every story or read certain characters as representatives of "God's will." The stories in this collection are *not* intended to be used this way. The action of the characters is not a hidden explanation of God's action, even though the reflection after the story touches on something we believe about God. I trust that God's Spirit is at work in our responses to the story, whether we can name those responses or not. I think that God moves within us and among us when we discuss a story, and when we simply offer a prayer, silently or aloud.

Growing with Family and Friends – Stories of Communion

The theme of *communion* or *love* takes us into the world of a child's relationships. Family and friendship offer both opportunity and dilemmas for every child. Many stories in this collection explore the dynamics of family life and the ups and downs of friendship. Parents interviewed often noted that, when talking about these stories, they began to hear more about the struggles their children faced with friends and schoolmates. These parents commented that they were glad for the occasions to let their children know that children are not the only ones who face challenges in relationships. A father noted that "the animal characters seem like a safer way to bring up issues with kids than using 'real' people as characters."

Introducing Fergie the Frog

Fergie the Frog is the first character I developed when I worked with children who lived in small communities where extended family life was strong and neighbours were familiar to each other. Fergie is a little brother, part of a frog family that lives by the side of a swamp. Fergie has a big brother, a best friend, parents, and a community of neighbours whose lives borrow both from human relations and from animal habits. So Fergie goes to school and to "Frog Scouts." He talks to the birds and the beavers. He eats peculiar food like "macaroni and fleas," designed to make a child laugh! In this imaginative world, I seek to give children an arm's-length look at their own families and neighbourhoods. The situations are close enough to everyday experience that children nod in acknowledgment. But the "froggishness" of life in the swamp is funny and strange enough that a child doesn't feel singled out. A thoughtful child will lead reflection in the direction that is appropriate to the moment. After reading some of Fergie's stories, one family reported:

> Conversations would start at random. Sometimes a phrase or situation would spark it. Our kids loved the varied menus the frogs ate. They seemed to sense the stories would take a humorous twist now and then. Often conversations about ridiculous situations stirred their deeper thoughts.

Fergie has proven to be a great favourite of young children. He represents their world that is centred on home but includes a gradually expanding circle of other children and other adults. Fergie's community includes "bully" frogs and friends who are different – garter snakes, turtles and toads. Fergie is a character who is likely to get into a spot of trouble now and then. Sometimes he doesn't listen to the advice his parents give. His struggles with his big brother reflect the kinds of squabbling and resentment that often arise between siblings. Fergie gets mad and hops away from home upon occasion. He doesn't always understand why parents make rules. He doesn't always understand his friends, either. The woodland creatures in Fergie's world also suffer interference from human beings from time to time. This dimension offers children the chance to reflect on the impact of human life on the vulnerable animals who have become their story friends and who are also part of God's creation.

In the midst of Fergie's community, then, children begin to examine their own power, its limits and its consequences in relationships. Several children I interviewed loved to imagine themselves as frogs, swimming "forever" or "hopping over everybody's heads." Frogs seem to symbolize freedom of action for many children. However, reflection on Fergie's relationships soon brings to the surface the complexities of being part of a community. Parents have told me that Fergie's stories often elicit the first stories the parents have heard about their children's painful encounters with friends at school:

> Our oldest boy, age 7, really related to the story *You Can Count on Fergie*. Ken is a very dependable child and found the questions following the story difficult. He is going through the stage where his best friend has many "best friends" and is therefore not a very dependable playmate. Ken's having trouble accepting that others are not the same as he is. As Ken put it, *"How come my friend can count on me and yet I cannot count on him?"*

A child's experience building and testing friendships is often invisible to parents, yet it leaves deep impressions on the child's self-esteem. When I interviewed children about what makes a good friend, over and over again I heard some story about being trustworthy. "A good friend remembers when they promised to come over," noted eleven-year-old Linda, who had found some of her playmates to be not so reliable. "A good friend gives other people chances to do better – like I give Ron chances to play with us," another young boy commented. As eight-year-old Eric summed it up, "A good friend makes a place for you." The theme of communion in a child's faith means knowing where you fit – in the family, with friends and with God – and knowing that your place is secure.

Fergie's adventures also call on him to act as a good friend. Sometimes he proves more trustworthy than at other times. This dimension of his stories also strikes a chord with children. When asked how to be a good friend, children readily proposed ideas about welcoming newcomers, helping somebody with a problem and sharing toys. The desire to be a good friend lives in tension with a child's self-interest, however. Children were quite candid about how hard it is to share the things they like. Trying to make up with friends after a conflict was also a challenge to my interview subjects. "I pretend like it never happened," said seven-year-old Anne when I asked how she responded to a friend who let her down quite often. Here we see an example of the struggle between self-respect, on one hand, and the desire for close relationships, on the other. In my study, children as young as five had begun to recognize the qualities in themselves and in their peers that make good friends. Naming and claiming these qualities can be an important moment when reflecting on the foibles of Fergie's friendships. It also provides an opportunity to talk about what it means to be the friends of Jesus and to follow Jesus' example.

Reflection on the ups and downs of Fergie's relationships gives storytellers the chance to hear about disappointments in friendships and anxieties in family relations. Children need an opportunity to voice their feelings about important relationships, because those feelings will often reveal a doubt about self-worth. When we feel that we don't matter to friends or family, we need both personal attention and faithful assurance. A story entitled *Fergie Gets a Surprise* explores the worry that some other child in the family is the favoured one. In my pastoral work, I often hear adults agonizing over the lingering certainty that their parents always loved another sibling more. Whether we are siblings or parents – or both – we should be realistic enough to recognize that favouritism does express itself in some families. Denying the feelings that result doesn't help. However, affirming what's special and lovable about a worried child is an important response in the face of self-doubt. Growing up with God means trusting God's love "for me" when it seems that no one else cares. Many reflections in this book invite children to trust in the enduring presence of God and God's generous love in the midst of self-doubt.

Fergie's stories raised an interesting comment from a church educator working with children in a multicultural congregation. The children in her program came from six or seven different homelands and all were newcomers to Canada. She said to me that Fergie had great appeal in this diverse group because "nobody has green skin." Fergie and his family belonged to all the children, whatever their own family's origin. Illustrated editions of *The Adventures of Fergie the Frog* have been translated into Spanish and Korean, while stories in English have found a home among Frog Clan children of the Nishga'a in Northern British Columbia. This character seems to speak to many children from many different cultural communities. There are advantages to being green!

Meet Sherman the Hound Dog

A second family setting is developed in the stories featuring Sherman the Hound Dog. Sherman is beloved of many children, partly because his antics remind them of family pets, but also because he lifts up some of the sad times and disappointments children face. Sherman belongs to a pair of children, Lucy, age seven, and Mark, age nine. Parents have a much lower profile in these stories than in Fergie's froggie world. In Sherman's collection, I am interested in examining how children come to conclusions about the world in dialogue with each other, and how those conclusions have consequences in relationships. For example, Sherman deals with other dogs – and cats! – in the neighbourhood. He reflects on why dogs "hate" cats and what a "real dog" is supposed to do. Here children begin to reflect on the differences they notice among their peers and whether or not those differences are important.

I was surprised in my interviews with children that sometimes the most obvious differences to *my* mind were not those raised by the children themselves. I expected children to comment on gender or ethnic differences among their classmates and friends. More often I heard observations about who was short or tall, who the fastest runner was, or what school certain friends attended. This is a reminder that children's perspectives are rooted in their daily experience. Value judgments are learned as children grow and absorb the comments and expectations of others around them. Storytellers who hope to encourage respect for human differences will find interesting dialogue partners in young children. Discussing stories about differences will help parents take note if, or when, a child's evaluating of differences among people takes on new emphases during elementary school years. Developing a regular family pattern of discussing such themes can help hold up God's love for all people in the face of social influences that devalue others.

Favourite stories featuring Sherman call up the difficult edges of childhood. Children interviewed often chose *Name Blame* as a story they liked. In this story, Sherman gets called names by several characters and ends his day feeling quite unhappy. When I discussed this story with children in Britain, many responded by telling me names they hate to be called. Very often these were pet names that parents used. Children are easily embarrassed by teasing names, including those meant affectionately. Time and again, children reported how they feel when they're called nasty names – sometimes "mad" but more often "sad." As four-year-old John put it, "I know what Sherman felt like when he went under the bed." John wasn't the only one, either. One Sunday after I told this story in worship, a mother approached me. She commented that I must have been at her house that week. Listening to the story, she had heard her own tired and angry voice blurting out something at her child. She thanked me for the story because it helped her see the unintended consequences of her own mood upon her child. She said she was going to apologize to her son over lunch that day.

Another popular story is called *When Sleeping Dogs Lie*. Children hear Sherman tell a lie and then watch the consequences unravel. Whenever I tell this story, children nod in recognition at the awkward feelings evoked when someone lies to cover up something. Exploring the feelings a little further, one parent heard a surprising insight from her seven-year-old:

> I was surprised by Ken's response to the question of why it's important to tell the truth. I expected him to say, "Because you could get in trouble." But he said, "Because if you blame the other person, they might get in trouble and not you. And you're the one who did it." I felt very pleased he thought of the impact on others first.

Exploring the theme of lying with children will push adults to grapple with a child's logic. Even knowing that lying is wrong, a child may nevertheless lie about something, especially about having done something else wrong. The child is trying to maintain relationship with a cherished adult by hiding a problem. The child cannot yet anticipate that the cherished adult may be more upset by the lie itself than by the behaviour denied in the lie. Sherman's story offers adults the opportunity to listen to a child's thinking and begin from there to help a child develop the courage to tell the truth, even risky truth.

Dealing with anger is another theme that interested children. *Temper Tantrum*, another favourite, recognizes how easy it is to hurt somebody who has hurt us. A mother of two commented that this story "generated the most animated and honest and enthusiastic responses.... We have our share of sibling confrontation!" Children do not find it easy to strategize about how to act when they feel angry and hurt. Retaliation was the response most often identified – "I'd hit him back!" or "I'd break one of her toys!" Such comments are common even when children sense that "hurting back" increases the likelihood of being hurt again, or of facing discipline. Talking through possible ways to handle anger at a quiet and calm story time can increase a child's repertoire of responses. For example, in the story *Who's Sorry Now?* Sherman acts as a peacemaker between Mark and Lucy, offering a small drama that connects with Jesus' teaching about forgiving and making peace.

Closely linked to the tug-of-war in retaliation is the challenge children face when asked to share what is theirs. In the story *How Big Is This Family?* Sherman and Lucy do not want to share their bedroom with a visiting aunt. During my interviews in Scotland, groups of children were eager to illustrate when and how they had to share their space at home. They offered examples in which brothers or sisters seemed to get a better deal, which is the situation presented in the story. Family life is built on sharing, of course, as is so much Christian action and service. Because children respond to issues of fairness so keenly, hearing them out on perceived unfairness is important so that resentment does not fester unexpressed.

Sherman's stories also open up the themes of loneliness and being left out. The poignancy of these feelings increases in a child's life, paradoxically, while that child is developing a wider range of relationships. As children grow to value friendships and activities more and more, so too will they feel emptiness, rejection and loss more keenly. From a faith perspective, it is important to affirm a child's value to God at moments when self-worth is in doubt in other relationships.

Growing in Confidence and Wisdom – Stories of Agency

It is also worthwhile thinking strategically with a child about what can be done in the midst of a lonely time or when relationships sour. A child's power to act is intricately involved in the forming and reforming of relationships. Helping a child identify and evaluate possible ways to build or rebuild friendships can develop a sense of faith in action. Assurance that God will never let us down can give us courage to take a risk on a new friendship. The third character whose stories are included in this collection often links the themes of agency and communion, when actions have challenging consequences.

Meet Jackie Rabbit

The adventures of Jackie Rabbit move a child from the familiar worlds of home and school into the world of systems and responsibilities. Jackie Rabbit starts her working life as a circus rabbit, being pulled out of sleeves. Her story cycle begins as she runs away from the circus, a tongue-in-cheek reversal of an old theme. In each story that follows, she is faced with finding a job or trying something new. Although young children do not face this exact situation, they become aware of the significance of work as they observe parents who must work – and sometimes have a hard time finding work. This theme was a lively one for me as a seven-year-old, when my father's business closed. I worried silently about what would happen to our family until one day I demanded to know, "Are we poor?" That question startled my mother. Rather than assuming children do not yet need to enter the world of economics and employment, I am convinced it is wiser to invite children to understand what it means to work and how parents' jobs affect how parents feel on some tiring or frustrating days!

Jackie Rabbit lives in a village "peopled" mainly by squirrels, porcupines and other animals who do human-like tasks. The villains of Jackie's stories are represented in animals, such as foxes, that would naturally present a threat to rabbits. Jackie is very much an agent in her world, putting herself on the line to try new things. Sometimes she is surprised by success. Sometimes she is disappointed by failure. She makes choices – and she makes mistakes. She has to keep thinking about what she *can* do when faced with things she can't do. Over the years, Jackie Rabbit has been a great favourite with young girls who still face obstacles not of their own making in this world. The need for girls to have female heroines in literature is widely recognized, and so for some female listeners, Jackie provides a courageous model of perseverance in the face of difficulty.

In *Story Project* interviews, I also met several young boys who enjoyed Jackie's stories very much. As I talked with these boys' parents for further insight, I learned that their sons were facing significant new challenges, entering new schools or changing activity groups. One mother recalled that her eight-year-old son was very interested in talking about Jackie's choices and why she would choose one job over another. He was soon to enter a new and bigger school. Jackie's appeal emerges as children begin to face situations on their own and have to think hard about making choices independently.

Parents might consider using Jackie Rabbit stories to talk with their children about safe and unsafe choices. Sometimes Jackie, out of stubbornness, makes an unwise decision. By the end of the story she learns about the foolishness of her choice. The consequences are never too dire – this is make-believe, after all. Of course, choices that our children make sometimes risk dangerous outcomes. Rather than shy away from these possibilities, I hope that parents and children can talk through the risks of danger so that children learn to recognize when they need help and where to go safely and wisely to find help. Fear and wisdom walk hand in hand for a person of faith. So do caution and courage. Times of reflection on choices and consequences can help children avoid needless risk but at the same time help them develop prudence and confidence when they find themselves in an unexpected situation.

I began to write Jackie Rabbit stories in 1980, long before I was aware of the changing economic realities young people face in the marketplace of the new millennium. Now I see that Jackie can help children develop a spiritual life to support them as they move into a world where most jobs won't last a lifetime. All of us now expect to change the work we do several times in a lifetime. This will mean learning new things, moving to new places, facing new situations. Jackie Rabbit's constantly changing world may help children to recognize the gifts and abilities God gives them to rely on. Conversation that reflects on a child as *agent* in God's world encourages children to approach new situations with confidence in God's presence to help them learn from mistakes and start again.

Faith on the Front Doorstep

In the introduction to this book, we met Kate, a seven-year-old girl in my parish who arrived at my house with a story to tell and a problem to solve. Kate's older sister had been saying "mean things" about Kate at school. A little conversation opened up the themes of agency and communion, power and love. I asked Kate what mean things Carrie had been saying. It turned out that Carrie had been telling tales on Kate, reporting that Kate had been mean to other children, including Carrie: pushing them around and calling them names. When I asked Kate if these "mean things" were so, she looked at her knees and nodded silently. Chickens had come home to roost for Kate. She had exercised her power to speak and to act – and now faced unhappy consequences. She discovered that her actions put her relationships in jeopardy. She worried what the teachers would think. She knew already that other children were reluctant to be her friends. The school community which she longed to be part of was suddenly less secure, less welcoming. What would you have said to Kate?

It's tempting when children tell us their stories to meet those stories with one of our own: "Why, Kate, I remember when I was a little girl…." Adults can build bridges with children by sharing childhood memories – but not when the child presents an immediate issue to consider. To bring up my own childhood at that moment could easily have shut off Kate's truth telling. Once Kate acknowledged that the "mean things" being said were accurate reports, we just sat for awhile. Then I suggested she might try doing the exact opposite of those mean things. Walk away when she was angry instead of hitting back. Bite her lip instead of calling someone a name. As you might imagine, doubt filled her eyes. I could tell, however, that she already felt ashamed by what she had revealed. So my strategy at the time was to help her think about other options for her own action. We talked about situations when her big sister really bugged her. Tentatively, Kate began to describe what she could do. I hoped to lift up the biblical models of "turning the other cheek" and "doing to others what we would like them to do to us" in ways that gave her some concrete choices to consider.

This example relates to another insight from the research of Robert Coles. In his book *The Moral Intelligence of Children,* Coles speaks about the importance of the Golden Rule in Jesus' teaching: "In everything do to others as you would have them do to you" (Matthew 7.12). He observes that children can and often do use this teaching as a measure to evaluate what they think of as "good."[7] An opportunity to discuss how to respond with generosity or self-restraint when you feel like hitting or yelling back begins to weave Jesus' teaching into children's ethical reflection. It is important to talk about why the desire to retaliate is not the wisest choice, or the most faithful. Coles' work demonstrates how much children have to say about the moral choices they face. Even if we haven't discussed such choices very often at home or at church, children are willing to present their ideas to adults who listen with respect.

One evening I was supervising a dance at church for children aged ten to twelve. At one point, three girls cornered me. They had a complaint about another girl at the dance. "Dana is a real pain. She is telling the boys not to dance with us. Saying bad things about us." I asked what they wanted me to do. "Make her be our friend." I knew that Dana's family was filled with conflict and grief. She was having a very hard time. I proposed a version of the same solution I offered to Kate. "Treat Dana the way you want her to treat you. Be her friend. She really needs friends right now." They nodded and went back to the group. Twenty minutes later they circled around me again. "It's not working," the leader declared. "Dana is still being a pain." I swallowed a chuckle as I explained that it might take more than twenty minutes to build a friendship. The evening drew to a close and I forgot about this exchange. Four months later I was at a community function. Once again these children sought me out. The leader of the pack spoke. "It worked, you know." I had no idea what she meant. "Dana. She's our friend now. We all like each other. It worked, just like you said." I had to give Jesus the credit, of course. Reading Coles' interviews with children reminded me of this episode. Discussing with children possibilities on which they can act helps them grow in moral decision making and practical "discipleship."

Creating Possibilities in Conversation

Opening up conversations with children seeks an invitation into their world. Consider yourself a guest in a child's story as that child describes what happened, what feelings and meaning have been claimed from a situation. Parents who tested *The Story Project* material found that new subjects for conversation would surface, generally after using the stories with the corresponding questions and prayers for two or three weeks. Some parents were quite surprised to hear how deeply their children thought about things, especially complex situations in the family or situations in the news. As one parent put it,

> One of the great things about these stories is that they encourage children while they are still young to talk about their experience and questions, even if they are not naturally talkers. Our youngest brought up how he had felt left out on the playground days after an incident. I was amazed about how much more must go on inside him that I don't hear about!

Most families in *The Story Project* found that children engaged in the model of reflection quite openly and even eagerly after a little while. Parents learned that the willingness to discuss situations grew as children came to enjoy the stories:

> In the beginning the children felt awkward responding to the questions. Their responses were often one-word answers and lots of "I don't know"s. But the second time through the sto-

ries, they became more willing to discuss issues like friendship and forgiveness, being different, and their own vulnerabilities.

In a few situations, however, conversation proved difficult. Sometimes very young children were not interested in the questions, only in the stories. In a couple of families, a child had trouble articulating feelings, a difficulty linked to the child's developmental challenges. In such a situation, a particular child's needs and abilities deserve primary consideration. Simply using the reflection section at the end of each story allows children who are reluctant for any reason to talk about the stories to think further on their own, at their own pace and according to their interest.

Using the stories and reflections with groups of children often involves some talkative partners and some silent partners in discussion. By nature, some children process their feelings and conclusions internally. Others, either by personality or age, are more willing to share ideas and tell stories. At first when using this model, both parents and teachers received many "right answers," cautious responses raised from a child's expectations rather than life experience. "God" and "Jesus" are often the first answers a child provides to any faith-related question, even if the name doesn't fit the question. With such answers a child seeks approval from an adult and tests whether the adult is really interested in what the child has to say. The questions included with each story in this collection attempt to elicit feelings and further storytelling, rather than right answers. It may take time for a child to trust that a heartfelt opinion or feeling is truly welcome, especially if that child anticipates disapproval. Adult storytellers need patience and hospitality to wait for genuine responses and to encourage the feelings and ideas behind short or stock answers. Given time and a welcoming attitude, most children have responded to the invitation to talk about what matters to them and to ask the questions that are on their minds.

Listening by Heart

Significance arises when we weave together the feelings evoked in a situation and the conclusions we draw about what has happened. Whether the feelings were happy or sad, whether the conclusions were correct or skewed, if we found an event significant as a child, we will polish the memory and hang onto the meaning we've made of that time, often for many years. Hearing a child relate an episode of significance is therefore an important occasion. When we listen by heart, we listen for the feelings, named or unnamed. We listen for the logical connections a child is making.

It is very common for children between the ages of four and nine to make logical connections which fit in their world view but which are not in fact accurate. Children can overemphasize their responsibility for causing things to happen. For example, when confronted with divorce in the family, many children worry and wonder what they did to cause the problem. Some children believe for many years that if they only can do or say the right thing their separated parents will be reunited. One mother pointed to this reality:

> Children get information from all different sources. They don't always hear it the way you think they should. The stories provide a much-needed opportunity to discuss these things, to listen and hear how the children are hearing and processing things. Then I can lend some affirmation or some guidance.

Between ages four and nine, children do not know how to interpret accurately the motives or feelings of others, especially adults. They can be very vulnerable to friends who let them down, and they are sensitive to critical comments from parents and teachers. At the same time, these same children may not recognize the consequences of their own actions. They will retaliate in anger many times before it begins to dawn on them that retaliation makes matters worse. When we listen to a child tell us about something that happened, we may be tempted to correct the child's thinking quickly in a response of genuine compassion – to spare the hurt feelings or needless anxiety. However, it is important to listen long enough and ask enough leading questions to reach the heart of the child's concern. That concern may be rather different than what an adult anticipates, because we hear through the filter of our own childhood memories or understand within the wider framework of adult experience.

A grandparent related an example of children's logic at work. His six-year-old granddaughter came home from her Grade 1 class at the end of her first week and announced she was finished with school. A little enquiry unearthed her expectation that she was supposed to know everything presented in her class already. In just a few days, school had shown her what she didn't know and she was afraid to return. It's easy to imagine how such an expectation gets set up in a bright child who knew how to count and how to say her ABCs before she went to kindergarten. Kindergarten had held few surprises for her, but Grade 1 proved to be another matter! She needed to share her fear and then to talk with her parents about what it means to learn. Once she was clear on the concept, she was glad to go back to school.

Feelings are an important indicator of the meaning a child attributes to specific events or to series of events and relationships. The stories in this collection can be used to invite children to express their feelings. "How did you feel in the middle of that story?" is a simple question to open up a little conversation. "Has something like that ever happened to you?" can offer the next step to hear what's on a child's mind. When I'm talking about these stories with young children, I have learned to stay away from a speculative question like "Why do you suppose that happened?" Although children from age three or four onward are full of their own "Why?" questions, their ability to predict motives or explain causes is still limited. Better, therefore, to stick to concrete reflections. "I wonder what Fergie can do now?" invites concrete thinking. Then it's not too big a step to talk about "what I can do" when a story creates a feeling or evokes a memory. An adult storyteller can help children develop their ability to interpret the world and understand others by offering suggestions. "I wonder if Jackie felt…." Let the children differ with you, however. Making proposals and then exploring suggestions will engage children in the concrete thinking of which they are capable – and give them some new ideas to consider.

The significance of regular conversations with young children came home to me during one of my interviews for *The Story Project*. I talked with a five-year-old girl who lived with her mother, a single parent. In a very short period, Claire had faced some significant changes in her important relationships. One of her grandparents had been seriously ill. The father figure in her life left abruptly. Her closest friend moved away. I wondered how she understood herself in the midst of all this. Claire acknowledged that she was both mad and sad at her friend who was now too far away to visit. I was surprised, however, by the strength of her self-confidence. She took delight in telling me about her trip to the water slides and how she braved a difficult chute. At one point she threw her hands upward in delight as she relived the thrill of her adventure. "I'm amazing!" she declared, a big smile on her face. I was impressed by her joy and conviction. Throughout that difficult year, this child maintained her sense of place in the world.

Claire's mother explained that the two of them talked a lot. She tried to let Claire know that she too felt the sadness of their losses. In our discussion, this mother asked whether I could develop some stories to show children why parents act the way they do. However, I think that she has already found the wisest solution: that is, sharing with her daughter how she feels about the situations they face together. Children do not readily credit parents with feelings because children's feelings are so central to their own way of understanding life.

Parents can begin to expand a child's appreciation for the feelings of others when using these stories by proposing how secondary characters might feel. For example, after a Fergie the Frog story, imagine the response of a parent frog character. "I bet Father Frog was really tired after work when this happened." "I wonder if Mother Frog was really scared when Fergie ran away." However, if you move from how characters feel to your own feelings, state such feelings very simply and claim them as your own. Otherwise children instinctively feel responsible for a parent's feelings. Let both parent and child offer their feelings to God in prayer as separate concerns that seek God's listening ear. The child's appreciation for God's presence with us in challenging times will grow. Claire's mother noted that her daughter expressed "a more personal relationship with God" as they talked about stories in this collection. Her faith in God helps Claire know she is loved and "amazing," even in a disruptive time.

Young children know their own stories by heart. Their feelings are closely connected to the meaning of events they remember and to the conclusions they draw about their own power and ability. But how, then, do they know God? If feelings are linked closely with meaning in a child's world, how do children view the meaning of God's presence in the midst of things they feel very deeply? In the next chapter, we will listen to the questions about God, God's power and God's love that were raised by children in *The Story Project*.

Once again, listen with your heart.

Chapter 2

Landscapes of Wonder

Lisa, the four-year-old daughter of a friend, insisted on saying grace before dinner one evening. "Thank you, God, for our food. The kangaroos are coming. Amen." No, my friend assured me, kangaroo was not on the menu! A few weeks later during worship, the kangaroos appeared on the horizon again. When the congregation prayed aloud the words of the Lord's Prayer, "Thy kingdom come," Lisa boldly announced, "The kangaroos are coming."

Adults are often amused by the ways in which children hear religious language. Perhaps we should also be amazed by the ways in which children's minds are working. Lisa's four-year-old vocabulary did not recognize kingdoms, so she substituted for herself another rather mysterious word that could make sense of adult speech rhythms. For young children, kangaroos are delightful creatures whose powerful hopping is a wonder. Often known through storybooks, television, or perhaps a trip to the zoo (at least outside Australia!), a kangaroo is both familiar to a child and yet a subject of mysterious possibilities. So, if something mysterious is coming, let it be a kangaroo!

Talking about God draws us into the territory of wonder where many things make us marvel, but not everything can be explained. Young children are guided by a spirit of wonder that many adults have surrendered in the "information age." Children work with the world they know to propose a vision of the wider world about which they wonder. Jewish philosopher Abraham Heschel sees wonder at the core of our encounters with God. Wonder itself is not faith, Heschel suggests. In wonder we sense God's approach to us. Faith is "the question of what to do with the feeling for the mystery of living, what to do with awe, wonder or fear."[8] *The Story Project* explored with children the questions and ideas that emerged for them out of their wonder about God and the world.

Led through the landscape of childhood wondering, adults have something to learn, or perhaps to relearn. Children encounter God's mystery day by day. Their questions about God and about the world take nothing for granted as they explore both sides of wonder. They are *fascinated* by so many things – by the design on a butterfly's wing or the way escalator stairs disappear. They are also *puzzled* by the same things, asking whether all butterflies are exactly the same or if all those moving stairs pile up in the basement. As young minds are both amazed and puzzled, God's spirit is stirring. We can help children learn to claim their wonder as God's invitation to faith. At the same time, our own appreciation for God's world may be awakened in fresh ways. As Heschel says, "Life without wonder is not worth living. What we [adults] lack is not a will to believe, but a will to wonder."[9]

When I worked with children on the Isle of Iona, I often heard them speak of their wonder. A three-year-old girl sat beside me during worship in the abbey one morning. When the worship leader spoke through the microphone, the young girl's eyes opened wide. She whispered, "The sky is talking." In that moment, the church became a space in which she could wonder. The framework of worship will help her connect her wonder to God. Another day I interviewed a five-year-old boy who had drawn me his favourite thing about his week on the island. I saw an odd figure at the top of the page and a similar, smaller picture at the bottom. "Tell me about your picture," I prompted, unsure of what I was seeing. "This is God," he said, pointing to the top figure. "And this is me." He indicated the smaller figure. "I just wanted to sit and think about God while I was here." The holy space of the abbey created a response of wonder in this young boy. His favourite part of his holiday was thinking about God!

These are candid comments from very young children. These children demonstrate the double track of wonder, marvelling and musing. As they discover themselves relating to a world much larger than themselves, they begin to reflect on what is happening. Because both these children are growing up in families that attend worship together, they have begun to connect their experiences of the world to God. And so their faith grows. But because they work things out by moving from the familiar to the unfamiliar, puzzles emerge, puzzles that often make adults smile. Still, we need to appreciate that these children are placing themselves in the middle of God's mystery. It is important for children simply to name their place as they see it.

Heschel distinguishes between faith and wonder in a way that honours the musings of children. Though faith is not the same as wonder, faith is fed by an appreciation of the wonders all around us. Faith is trust in the God who has created the wonders of this world and given us the capacity to marvel at them. Natalie, a four-year-old I met in Scotland, demonstrated this as we walked to the beach one morning. As we trudged up a hill, she suddenly stopped and looked at me. She gestured at the sky. "God isn't just up there, you know. He's down here with us." She pointed at herself. "He's in my heart. He's in your heart." Then she paused and looked into the field. "He's in the sheep's heart." Another pause. As she looked at the ground, she nodded. "And he's in the stone's heart, too." Natalie knows the world as a landscape of wonder. She also is learning to trust that God is present with her in every detail of that world.

As I listened to Natalie, I was impressed by how clear she was in her own mind. She helped me look afresh at the world in its beautiful detail. The wonder that children inspire in adults arises from their candour. They speak so frankly about their encounters with the world. They give voice to what they see and to what they don't. Children often speak of God in such candid ways. Their insights and their questions present us with wisdom about life, as you will hear in the conversations throughout this chapter. That wisdom grows from naming what is and what isn't. Yet children need adults as companions to figure out the significance of what they see and to choose how to respond. For while they can and will name what they see often more directly than adults, young children are only learning to understand why and how things happen.

An appreciation for the double edge of wonder helps to explain why the stories in this collection eventually encourage children to voice their marvelling and their musing about God. This storytelling model invites deliberate consideration of the meaning of our lives. How can we fit the various pieces of our experience together in light of what we think about God? When the pieces don't seem to fit together, then how do we reach out to God? Who is God for us then? Such questions often have no easy answer. Yet children are interested to explore them, often in direct and refreshing ways. A parent in *The Story Project* commented, "I have been impressed with the universality of the stories, the power of narrative to evoke my children's feelings. These stories make the children think and give them permission to wonder and question." A mother of three children added,

> I used the reflections and questions and found them excellent ways to start conversations. My five-year-old had a few challenging questions, but since my eight- and eleven-year-olds usually listened also, I found they would provide ideas. Between the three of them, they usually came up with an appropriate answer.

By using the faith-focused reflections and questions after each story, adults help children consider faith in God as part of everyday life. Research on the influence of family religious practice on faith development has shown that conversations about faith at home are one of the strongest influences on children as they grow. When at least one parent talks about God with a child, or when prayer or ritual forms a regular part of family life, the roots of a child's faith in God are nourished. By exploring both the feelings and the questions these stories evoke for the child, a family can develop familiar ways of speaking of God in the midst of events that matter. And in this holy territory of our living, God will meet us, and we will have new stories to tell.

As children grow to discover God as their mysterious and trustworthy companion, we can help them connect those imaginary "kangaroos" to the kingdom of God's redeeming love and honour their changing abilities to understand the world. The way a five-year-old or an eight-year-old speaks of God will not be their final language for their faith. As children develop the capacity for more complex reasoning, their ways of thinking and talking about their faith will change. Therefore, don't worry about correcting each idea a young child suggests. Phrase what you believe in simple statements and encourage children to talk about what they think for now. Pay close attention to what a child is feeling in the present moment. If we learn how to talk openly about our faith with children as they grow, there will be opportunities in the future to clarify and deepen our commitments. A mother of six-year-old twins offered this insight:

> Sometimes I just ask the questions and don't worry about whether or not I get a response or discussion right away. I hope that the question will stick with them and give them a chance to think and wonder, even if they aren't ready to discuss it yet.

Voices of Wonder

When adults draw alongside children to consider who God is and how we meet God in the world, we will often hear very puzzling descriptions from our young partners. Conversations with children who took part in *The Story Project* unleashed many interesting insights and questions. Their comments have been gathered into sections to help you anticipate the kinds of concerns that occupy children's wondering time in response to this collection. Four themes emerged in conversations with my young subjects:

— The wonder of it all – concern for the world as God's creation
— The landscape of life – God in the midst of our lives
— Holy, holy, holy – wondering about God
— Horizons of heaven – what lies beyond what we can see

In these conversations, I had to learn again to speak about God in the concrete terms of daily life that children use. This is not always easy for adults, because the language of our faith is filled with abstract concepts and figures of speech that do not yet make sense to young children. I listened for words the children themselves chose and used those words to explore their ideas. In the sections that follow, I have put in *italics* the concepts of Christian tradition that I recognized in what children said to me. The children were not yet ready to use these conceptual terms themselves. However, by relating these concepts to situations children described, I gained a sense of the fullness of their faith.

After we consider the children's input on these four themes, we will look at ways to respond to the really challenging questions that also puzzle parents and teachers. Children's ability to be direct about their ideas often identifies questions for adults to explore on our own terms, to deepen our own faithful understanding.

The Wonder of It All: Concern for the World as God's Creation

Some of the children who participated in *The Story Project* lived in large urban or suburban areas; others lived in small towns close to the ocean or in the midst of prairie grain fields. From the youngest to the oldest, they expressed a consistent view that God wants people to care for the earth. Their concern for the earth and for animals expresses a child's sense of connection with the world in its many parts. It is also the foundation of what Christian tradition calls *the doctrine of creation*. In early years, children readily learn to honour the earth and each creature as precious to God, our "Maker."

"God gives us everything," declared Eric, age eight. He added quite firmly, "God gives us the ozone layer." He knew that the ozone layer protects the earth and he connected that protection with God's protection. His mother noted that Eric thought a lot about one of Fergie's stories, *Fergie Cleans Up*. This story explores how human beings hurt the places where frogs live. Eric knew that climate change is destroying frog habitat around the world. There are fewer frogs than there once were. As Eric and his mother talked about this story, Eric sensed already that not everyone shares his concern. Here is a remarkable opportunity to connect a child's faith with family lifestyle decisions and discuss the cost of such faith-filled decisions. Even at eight, Eric knows the debate in the media over environmental protection. His commitment was clear. This kind of ethical conviction offers the chance for children to think specifically about what they can do to care for the earth as God's creation.

Older children had some pretty clear ideas about what caring for the earth means. Eleven-year-old Linda also understood caring for the earth as something God gives us to do. "We try to reuse stuff and recycle stuff," she explained, adding that she sometimes shared in cleaning up the church grounds and the schoolyard. "And if we see someone treating an animal badly, we tell them to stop." Her urgency on this point reflects another common concern for children, that animals are precious to God, too. Several younger children expressed this concern as they wondered whether animals go to heaven. When asked what she thought, Linda replied, "I think animals go to the same heaven we do." By age eleven, Linda also wondered "how we got alive, how we were created. I think about what the Bible says at the beginning," she added, admitting sometimes she had more questions than answers.

As children begin to study science, tensions often emerge between scientific theories about the history of the earth and the poetry of Genesis and the Psalms. I grew up in a time and place where this tension was not seen as a contradiction or a battle between authorities. I learned to trust God as our Maker whose Spirit moves in the intricacies of the world, in a child's heart as well as in a scientist's inquiry. This conviction guides the way I engage a child with Linda's questions. Children now grow up learning how human life makes an impact on the earth. If we help them think of the earth as God's beloved creation, science can be valued for and judged by its ability to maintain health and life for God's world. From the same perspective, we can judge and value other human actions for their faithfulness to God's desire to care for all life in its goodness.

By the time children are nine or ten, they can begin to learn how the Bible came to be a single book. They are now developing a sense of history. Understanding the generations of God's people who contributed to Scripture, first through oral storytelling and then by written text, helps them appreciate the faithfulness that has brought the Bible to us. God is known through this long and complex history. Learning about the human hands and voices we meet in Scripture also gives us the opportunity to talk about how we listen for God's "Word" in human words – and in the stirring of our own hearts. This is an important conversation to begin with children to prepare them for times when it is not easy to figure out what God is "saying" to us. Every child should know that God's people have always struggled to answer this question. In its variety of voices, the Bible tells us that God is faithful to us when we struggle to live according to our faith.

Children struggle to know God when things go wrong. Their deep connection to God's creation means they feel it deeply when some part of creation is hurt. Several parents remarked on how important it was for their families to mark the death of animals, both well-loved pets and wild birds and animals that met untimely ends. Such experiences raise natural sorrow, often a child's first taste of grief. Encouraging tears to flow is important so children learn that their tears are a natural and healthy part of grieving. Creating a burial ritual can help a child see dignity in death. Below, in the section on "Horizons of Heaven," you will find references to biblical passages that might bring some comfort at sad times.

Animal deaths may also raise questions about why sad things happen. These questions stretch everyone's faith, for in the end explaining "why" doesn't change sad reality. I wrote the story *Fergie Loses a Friend* to help children reach out to God in such a sad time, drawing on the Bible story in which Jesus weeps for his friend who has died. The time to talk about what happened may emerge after shock and strong feelings have subsided a little. Fergie's story might be helpful to read a few days or weeks after a child confronts the death of an animal. It is also helpful to read whenever a child knows loss – for example, when a good friend moves away.

The mother of six-year-old Bruce faced a surprising question on this topic shortly after Easter. Bruce noticed a dead black squirrel lying by the side of the road, likely a hit-and-run victim. "Mommy," he asked, "when will God raise up the squirrel?" She wasn't quite sure what to say. "What makes you think God will raise up the squirrel?" she asked, trying to keep the conversation going. "God has to raise him up, just like Jesus," Bruce declared. She marvelled at his conviction. A few days later she and Bruce were out in the back yard. A black squirrel scampered along a branch above them. "See, Mommy," Bruce announced, "God did raise up that squirrel. There he is." For her, this episode revealed how much Bruce absorbed of what he heard in church. She was also amazed at what deep trust Bruce had in God's power.

Children often express their wonder about God's creation through compassion for what gets damaged or injured. We might think of such compassion as the God-given gift to care, a gift of faith to be recognized, honoured and encouraged in children's lives. In the next section, the same emphasis on caring is named again by children as they describe God's connections to us in the midst of human life.

The Landscape of Our Lives: God in the Midst of Human Life

Children attend to God's interest and concern for human life in both a very broad sense and also in specific, personal ways. Eric surprised his mother in a comment following *Who's Sorry Now?* In this story, Sherman acts as peacemaker during an argument between Lucy and Mark. Eric commented that God doesn't want people to hurt other people or to fight with each other. His mother took another step. "Does God need peacemakers?" she asked. "Yes," Eric continued. "God doesn't want the world to be a weapon." Exploring a little further, Eric's mother realized that Eric was thinking deeply about stories he saw on the television news. Images of war had scared him. Amy, who is also eight, responded to the same story, saying that "they need peacemakers in Ireland," but she couldn't say why. Her father explained a little about the history of fighting between Protestants and Catholics there. Amy replied quite simply, "That's dumb." Children's perceptions of the wider world form an important topic for prayer, as we will see in the next chapter. Children can release both their fear and their hope to God on such world issues when they pray.

Exploring the kinds of concrete actions a peacemaker can take in the schoolyard will draw out the ethical choices people face in all kinds of conflict. Several children in the study recognized that "God wants us to forgive each other." Anna, a nine-year-old, added, "If people never forgave each other, it'd be a cruel world." As I listened to the older children in *The Story Project*, I heard many of them expanding their sense of God's desire for us as individuals to consider what God wants for the world. Conversations that connect our convictions about God with the way we treat our neighbours and with the times we stand up for our beliefs lay a foundation for faithful citizens of the future.

Their broad concern for peace in the world is linked to children's sense that God loves the whole world. Sandy offered her six-year-old perspective this way: "God has love for everyone in the world. He has the most of all. I only have enough love for some people." Her candour reminds us that young children already feel the struggle to live out the values encouraged at home and at church. Several stories in the collection raise different glimpses of the struggle children face to put God's love in action. Getting along with friends proved to be a lively way to enter this topic.

When he considered what God asks us to do with our friends, John, age four, declared firmly, "God asks us to play." At age four, children usually expressed the conviction that everyone could be a friend. But by age six, the need to discern "good friends" had emerged. Discussing what a friend can do to show God's love, children often named the importance of welcoming someone new: "Tell someone your name. Say hello." "Show them where to find stuff at school." Over and over again, children thought of small acts of kindness that would reflect God's care for each person: "When people feel sad, help them feel better." Nine-year-old Anna summed it up this way: "Be yourself, be a caring person, be grateful that you are what you are."

In these wide-ranging comments, we see the child's gift of wonder piecing various aspects of their world together with teaching about God. Affirming God's connection to all of life emerged consistently as children reflected on what happens around them. Questions and insights were also provoked by experiences that didn't measure up to what they believe God desires. Anna pointed out to me the problem of "saying sorry, but not really being sorry." Her voice imitated a fake apology – "Sor – RY! Then you know it's not real," she added. Another puzzle is presented by "bad people." Kent, age five, wondered, "Do bad guys have God in their hearts?" His mother offered the following reflection:

> I told him that I believe bad guys (meaning those who had broken the law) have lost touch with God and are more worried about themselves than what they do to others. I said that often people lose God from their hearts when bad things have happened to them growing up. I also told him that sometimes people find God in their hearts again when they're in jail and have time to think about what they've done.

Her response is a bit complicated for a five-year-old to understand fully, but I appreciate her willingness to say what she believes. She also pictures for her son the hope that someone's relationship to God can change for the better, a hope that expresses what Christian faith calls God's *grace*.

What impresses me in the insights of both these children is their ability to reflect on life in a wide perspective. Anna makes an example of something that has happened to her, perhaps many times. She is not satisfied with this behaviour. Kent is evaluating what he observes, perhaps on television, perhaps in the news, but not from his direct experience. In very concrete ways, these children are taking the measure of what Christian tradition refers to as *sin*, when people somehow fall short of what God truly desires for us. This capacity in children to think deeply about what happens around them is stirred up by a child's faith. It is the capacity to meet God in the midst of daily life, something that can nourish our faith for a lifetime.

I observed an interesting encounter between two friends in Scotland, nine-year-old girls who had "annoyed each other" all week during our group activities. Invited to draw her favourite part of our week together, Sarah drew a girl. "Who is this?" I asked. "Colleen," she announced, referring to the girl with whom she had argued every day, a girl who could reduce Sarah to tears with a single comment. I had observed Colleen patiently seeking out Sarah any time she stormed off in tears.

Nancy: Why did you draw Colleen's picture?

Sarah: Because she has been the kindest person in this place. Even though we annoyed each other. She was a little bit mean to me. And I was a little mean to her. But she was nice to me, too.

Nancy: Sarah, that's a very kind thing to say. Would you tell Colleen what you just said to me?

Sarah: (Pause) Sure.

I invited Colleen to come and listen. Sarah repeated to Colleen exactly what she had said to me, thanking Colleen for still being nice even after they had annoyed each other. Sarah's public gesture of *reconciliation* was not lost on Colleen. She later expressed to me a sense of surprise and satisfaction that Sarah could say this in front of our whole group. Encouraging children to repair relationships is an important commitment if we take Christian teaching about reconciliation seriously. At nine, these girls won't use that word. Still, they find satisfaction in making peace and renewing their friendship.

During *Story Project* interviews, I also wanted to see how children's faith might be connected to their ideas about their own future. To the familiar question "What do you want to be when you grow up?" I added a question about how their choice could help God in the world. Anna responded that she wanted to be an author and illustrator. "Authors write books to make the world more interesting," she added. Her younger sister, Marcie, wondered about being a doctor or a librarian. She explained, "Librarians help people find the right books for them. Doctors help people, too." Here we see implicit values in these children's lives, shaped by a family's interest in books, and by a general sense that God intends us to help others. Linda, two years older than Anna, pondered the same questions. She thought that she would be either an artist or a dance teacher. "Artists," she affirmed, "draw pictures of what God created." This was a new angle on her interests, but she didn't hesitate to connect God's world with her own possibilities. Emma chose "veterinarian" as her future goal. "God loves the animals," she told me, "and when we look after them, they're like people."

At seven, nine and eleven, these girls have begun to connect their appreciation of God's love for the world with a sense of *vocation* or *service*: that is, what faith-filled human work contributes to God's world. This is a vital connection to encourage, so that children will continue to consider whether the possibilities for their future work fit into God's concern for creation. A five-year-old boy whom I interviewed on the same theme lived in a community that had just suffered a tragic fire in which a firefighter had been killed. Jack told me that he wanted to be a firefighter. "God uses firemen to blow out fires," he explained. He said that he felt sad "when a building gets hurt." His eight-year-old brother, Lorne, agreed. "Do you feel close to God when you're sad?" I asked. Lorne nodded, "Yes, very close." The responses of these children show once again the impact of current news on a child's thoughts and feelings. Sometimes the question we start with is not the real topic on the child's mind at that moment. From these comments, Lorne and I continued to talk about prayer, a conversation that will be explored in the next chapter.

Several children described God's presence with them in different ways. "God watches over us," said Lorne. This idea gave Jack and Lorne a bit of concern when they considered that God could see them "when we fight over toys." Kent, a five-year-old boy, added a different note: "God helps me think about what to do." He gave an example of a time when he knew he had to teach his younger brother something. "God protects me," said seven-year-old Marcie with assurance. But an eight-year-old wondered why we can't hide from God. This theological theme, *God's omnipresence*, is central to Christian faith. Often adults reflect the same tension that emerges in these children's responses. We trust that God "watches" us and responds to us in moments of need. At other times, however, God's presence everywhere can seem threatening or restrictive. This theme raises questions for deep reflection with children and in adult souls, too. How do we claim God's presence with us as energy for healthy living? What guidance can we count on? What limits will we face? Are we faithful to the limits God presents to us?

Recall the story about Penny in the introduction to this book. Penny, age eight, was musing on family plans to put up a real Christmas tree. She saw an ethical dilemma: "If Jesus came to bring us life," she wondered, "why do we kill Christmas trees to remember his birth?" Penny shows the concrete logic typical of her age. The contradiction in killing something to celebrate life struck her suddenly. As she begins to explore values, her mind is alert to right and wrong, what seems fair and unfair. In her comment we see the larger implication of her values breaking into her everyday world. She has claimed an insight from Jesus' life, one that suggests a limit on her own life. The opportunity to help a child consider how to reflect Jesus' life faithfully is not to be missed. That evening Penny's family decided to find a Christmas tree that came with a root ball packed in earth to plant in their yard after Christmas. In this way, they could celebrate Jesus' life with a living tree.

Children's ideas about God's presence with them in the world and about God's expectations of them point towards their underlying convictions about who God is and what God is like. I found myself both amused and amazed by the insights for the next section.

Holy, Holy, Holy: Wondering About God

Five-year-old Erin was busy colouring a picture of Fergie the Frog. She began to chuckle as she added lots of curly hair, rather like her own. We joked about hair on a frog and then I asked, "Do you think God has curly hair?" She gave that impatient frown children save for thick-headed grown-ups and said, "God doesn't have curly hair. God is not human, you know." Her definite tone surprised me. I had expected her to offer a concrete, human-like image for God, coloured by her imagination. Claire, also five, resisted describing God when asked what God is like, but she confirmed that she wonders "where God came from, what God does, and where God is."

Robert Coles' exploration of children's spiritual life helped me prepare to interview young children. He invited children to draw pictures of what they imagined God to look like. He was a bit surprised that both Jewish and Muslim children refused to draw anything, for they had already taken to heart the teaching of their traditions not to make images of God. Christian children he interviewed produced many drawings, however – some featuring Jesus, others featuring a version of an old man with a beard.[10] When I looked at the illustrations in Coles' book, I realized how much children are influenced by the depictions of God as a male figure found in Western art. Yet Christian teaching shares with Judaism and Islam the biblical caution about making "graven images" of the Holy One. In light of Coles' observations, I decided not to ask children to draw pictures of God. Instead I offered them opportunities to draw pictures of stories they enjoy. Then I asked open-ended questions about God that could be answered in a variety of ways: What is God like? How would you tell a friend about God? Sometimes these questions elicited physical descriptions, but just as often, children responded by talking about God's nature as loving or caring.

Young children draw many of their questions about God from their own experiences of the world. "Does God sleep?" asked five-year-old Jack. His mother recalled, "I asked what he thought and Jack replied that he thinks God sleeps for a few minutes at a time." In my interview with Jack, he announced, "God takes very short naps." The same little boy wondered how God stays up in the sky. For Chris, one year older, a similar idea was percolating. He thought God lived up in space and wondered "if the astronauts could see God or angels flying around." Chris also imagined that God might wear an air mask "because there's no air in space." While these little boys haven't been to space yet, certainly their sense of God's place in the universe must include the images of space seen in the media. For other young children, God takes on impressive proportions drawn from human life. Paul figured that God "is a nice guy, pretty fat, with grey hair and a beard." He also suggested that "God must have the biggest credit card in the world"! One of my students interviewed a seven-year-old girl who was convinced that God lived in New York. Although she had never been to New York, she knew it was a very big place with very important people. In these examples, children are expanding on what they know to be important to present God as very important, even most important.

When talking with young children about God, I resist the urge to correct their imagined pictures, trusting that in time they will find new ways to speak about God. John Hull, a professor of religious education, reports on conversations he had with his own young children in *God-talk with Young Children*.[11] His work stimulates great appreciation for a child's sense of humour. Hull discovered that sometimes a child would say outrageous or funny things to see how Hull himself would respond. He soon realized that just saying something crazy aloud and having a good laugh released the nonsense for the child. His children seemed to try some ideas on for size and then let them go if they were more funny than serious. However, if a child raises a peculiar idea about God that you find troubling, then suggest another word picture that helps you think about God in a different way. Trust the Holy Spirit to work in the tension between different ideas.

I certainly learned in my conversations that young children can distinguish qualities of meaning within their own use of language. Consider this exchange as I watched six-year-old twins, Alex and Mark, demonstrate a video game. They wanted me to be impressed by how quickly they became "supersonic" as their screen players ate up video villains.

Nancy: Is God supersonic, do you think?

Alex: NO! God is with real people. Those guys are just characters.

Mark: This game is just pretend.

Nancy: So God deals with real people, with you.

Mark: Yes.

Nancy: Would you like to be supersonic?

Both: YES!!

(A pause, and then we continued.)

Alex: God is like a star.

Mark: God is like a sun.

Alex: No. The sun is what gives earth life. God is a star.

These children are doing more than distinguishing between real and pretend. In the contrast between the sun and the stars, they seem to differentiate between what is familiar and what is more mysterious as they talk about God. The twins' parents noted that these boys love to talk about God. They are filled with questions. "Did God build our house? Where is God? Is God *here?*"

It is a challenge to respond to the very concrete focus of these questions with more than one-word answers! Look for short sections in the Psalms that paint word pictures of God's glory and God's presence. Poetry and hymns will appeal to a child's imagination at this age. I remember in my early years at church singing all four verses of the Trinity hymn *Holy, Holy, Holy* every Sunday. The lyrics paint a vision of the heavenly throne room taken from chapter 4 in the book of Revelation. I certainly couldn't have "explained" it, but Reginald Heber's word pictures of "cherubim and seraphim" and all those saints "casting down their golden crowns around the glassy sea" played on my tongue and in my imagination, encouraging me to wonder about God's mystery.

Older children in the study offered somewhat different language to describe what God is like. Anna, age nine, said, "God is in the room with you but you can't see him. He's in every room." Emma, also nine, agreed that "God is everywhere." When I asked if she thought God was like a parent, she added, "My mom does a lot of things in different places, taking care of people, and that's like God – God is everywhere." (Emma's mother is a minister!) Linda, at eleven, considered several descriptions: "God is like a friend you can trust. God is like a father who loves you. God cares for us like our parents. But we can't say if God is a girl or a boy." I invited her to say a bit more about that. "It's not really important," she continued, "but it would be nice to know."

The way Linda phrases her interest about God "as a girl or a boy" is important to note. I realized that "gender," as adults use the term, is too abstract a concept for children, even at age eleven. Children use concrete language as they ponder who God is and how God is with us. They think about girls and boys, a man and a woman, Mom or Dad without using the terms we find in Genesis, "male" and "female." These concepts generalize identity in ways young children do not. As a theologian, I hope children eventually surround very concrete human categories, which ancient Christian tradition teaches are too literal to describe God's mystery, with a more poetic appreciation of the many biblical names and metaphors for God. But this ability develops at a somewhat later stage in life, so I left my young subjects to wonder at their own questions.

Does God ever get angry? I wondered with Linda. Yes, she agreed. "Wars and polluting make God angry." Is God ever sad? I asked. "The same things that make God angry make God sad," said my young theologian. She has begun to sort out how God engages the world in a variety of ways, using concrete examples but in figurative ways. She added that God is sad when people get sick but that God does not make people sick. "It just happens." Linda has reached the age when she can wrestle with cause and effect and demonstrates already the ability to reflect on life's complexity.

A few children spontaneously connected God with Jesus, although not as many as I expected. Sandy, at seven, commented, "I think of him [God] as Jesus' dad or something." Nine-year-old Emma noted, "Jesus is special because he's God's real son. But everybody is God's children." Linda had begun to think through the miracle stories. "The story about fish and bread, it's kind of curious, how we got all those fish." She paused. "Kind of magic," she added, groping for words. One of the parents made an interesting point on this theme: "This project made me realize that we don't use 'Jesus' in our conversation much except at church, so this has been a good opportunity to bring Jesus more into our lives and encourage more awareness."

The teaching of Christian tradition relating God as "Maker" and "Father" to Jesus as "Son of God and Son of Man" is complex for the most mature minds. We all grope for words to express what the tradition calls Jesus' *divine nature*. As the comments above indicate, children begin to consider Jesus as "God the Son" based on their own experience of families. Jesus' *humanity*, the other central theme in the Church's teaching about the Christ, connects with a child's world and worldview. Several children I interviewed named the Christmas story as their favourite Bible story. The Christ child in the manger invites a child to wonder in the same way young children do when they first notice each other's presence in public. Slightly older children were impressed by Jesus' visit to the temple without his parents' permission (in Luke 2.41-51), more because they admired Jesus' bravado than because he names God as "his Father." They share a bit of rebellious longing to assert themselves! Thinking of Jesus' disciples as "his friends" and Jesus as "our friend" fits in with a child's growing interest in friends.

The identity, trust and support of a friend are concrete connections with Jesus that children understand.

As children learn the stories about Jesus, it is important to respect their questions as they wonder with us how to bring the whole mystery of his identity into words. Once again, however, seven-year-old Sandy keeps the mystery in perspective for us with typical candour: "I don't really think about God and Jesus all that much now. But I'll do that more when I get old, like my Mom and Dad's age." She observes the active life of faith her parents lead and expects that for herself. For now it's enough for her to think that "God takes care of you."

Still, a child's theological thinking can startle us. Take Chris, age six, who asked his mother, "When did God die?" With Chris we enter a topic that fascinates children: heaven.

Horizons of Heaven: What Lies Beyond What We Can See

His mother was taken aback. She assured Chris that God didn't die. He continued, "Why does God live in heaven if he's not dead?" Here is six-year-old logic at work. Chris had been told that when we die, we go to heaven. He had also heard that God lives in heaven. It is a very simple connection to conclude that if God lives in heaven, God must have died.

I had not expected *The Story Project* to raise so many questions and comments from children about heaven. But when encouraged to talk about what was on their minds, children made heaven a common topic. Alex and Mark piled up their questions: "Who's in heaven? What does heaven look like? Where *is* heaven?" Then they remembered that their grandfather had died two years earlier. "Mommy's daddy knows where heaven is." This conclusion was satisfying at that point. Lorne, two years older, pondered heaven and suggested, "Heaven must be a big place. There's dog heaven, bug heaven, people heaven...." Here we see children's instinct for connection with all God's creatures expressed. Paul added that he thought heaven would be a "nice place, a big place, with a least two thousand people." To a seven-year-old raised in a small town, two thousand people sounds like more people than he will ever encounter!

Some children picked up on heavenly imagery found in Scripture and in popular culture. "There's a big cloud." "Sidewalks might be made out of gold." "People sleep on their fluffy cloud pillows." Kent, age five, asked another provocative question: "Do people grow in heaven or not?" When asked what he thought, he figured that children probably would grow but that grown-ups probably wouldn't. Her impression of heaven as "a dark place with spirits in it" made Anne remember her grandfather who had died a year earlier. She told me two special stories about things they did together. Again, one topic leads a child to another, and in this case there were important family stories to tell.

Children's ideas about heaven reflect much of the art and poetry from Christian tradition. Some images come from the Bible, while others come from the imaginations of artists and authors. Children also see a collage of angels, clouds and even figures representing God in advertising, newspaper cartoons and television shows. It's no wonder children want to know what heaven is like. This curiosity will be increased if someone known to them, including a beloved pet, has died.

Events in community life will also be gathered up into a child's pondering. This mother named a common concern for many parents:

> Claire is always asking questions about life and actually a lot about death. From her other religious experiences she seems somewhat distressed about death and has begun to worry about me going to heaven without her.

This comment is a reminder of how important it is to draw out a child's feelings and the logic that interprets feelings. Children at Claire's age, six, do not understand clearly what makes things happen. The death of someone they know or know about can unleash fear that the same thing could happen to someone they love and depend upon. Talking this fear through with a child takes some care, both to address the fear in practical and faithful ways but also to respect that fear without increasing it. My grandmother died when I was five. I remember my parents telling me who my guardians would be if anything happened to them. I suppose I expressed some fear I might be left all alone, although I don't remember that feeling. I simply remember which aunt and uncle were standing on guard for me! Knowing who will take care of them *if* something happens is important to a child.

Sometimes a child's fascination with heaven simply tries to make literal sense of the metaphors adults use. In John 14.1-3, for example, Jesus describes God's "house" as having many "dwelling places." When my grandmother died, I imagined that she would have a house in heaven just like her house in my neighbourhood. I figured her house was sitting there on a puffy white prairie cloud so she could watch me playing. I was putting together the images of house, clouds and heaven as "up there" in a way that gave me comfort. The word pictures from John's Gospel can give a comforting assurance that in heaven, God has "prepared a place" for each of us.

Another biblical image of heaven is found in chapters 21 and 22 of the book of Revelation. Here heaven is a holy city, where there is no night, and where God lives among people to dry their tears and to welcome them. If your child is worried about heaven, why not draw a picture of the holy city together? This biblical vision is such a colourful scene. If someone dear to the child has died, you might draw a "map" of the holy city and mark the place where that special person has found a place. Assure the child that the Bible promises us that we are precious to God. Whatever happens, God will make a place for us to be safe in God's love.

The Bible also pictures God's "kingdom" as a party, a wedding celebration, and a banquet where there is enough food and enough space to welcome all God's people. This image may be hard to present at a time of tragedy, when a party is the farthest thing from anyone's mind. Still, it is a picture that can later reassure us that each precious person shares God's love and attention in "life everlasting." I sometimes speak of someone who has died "saving a chair for us" at God's banquet table. This is the kind of concrete image a child can visualize, and appreciate the promise of *resurrection* as a chance to meet again, blessed by God's love.

Many comments from children speak of their concern for animals that die. The Bible does not directly address this theme. However, there is a word picture in Isaiah 11.6-9 that can speak to their concern. The prophet writes about "the day of the Lord" and pictures animals living in peace together. The wolf and the lamb live together, a cow and bear graze side by side. In this way the prophet imagines the healing of all creation, as predators and prey at last coexist without harm. If we trust this picture of God's intent for the whole creation, then I think we can assure children that God will care for pets whom they have loved and lost. Those pets are somewhere on God's "holy mountain" where nothing can be hurt or destroyed.

By presenting the many different word pictures for God and for heaven found throughout the Bible, we help children develop new ways of thinking about God. These word pictures draw on a child's ability to imagine a safe and happy place. When one image of God's love doesn't quite fit our current situation, another will "speak" truth or "show" us God's promise that God's love will never let us go (Romans 8.38-39). Affirming that there are many ways to think about God's love and God's action is very important, for no single word picture and no single Bible story says everything. Talk of heaven ought to emphasize our hope in God and our trust in God's goodness and love. Handing our fears and sorrow over to God in prayer can also release troubled feelings that may arise in our conversations.

There are several good resources listed in the bibliography at the end of this book to help children of different ages cope with loss and death. Please consult these resources for help to explore specific situations that you face with your children.

Exploring Holy Ground Together

The Story Project conversations confirmed a hunch that emerged when I first began to write stories for children. When stories offer an authentic voice to children's feelings and questions about life, children find their own voices to present questions and stories of their own. When faithful adults use language about God's presence with us in the midst of life, children begin to speak of their experience of wonder, their convictions and their questions about God. A colleague shared with me a profound moment of the power this model can provide in a young life.

He spent some time as a summer camp director, working with campers mostly of Aboriginal heritage. Over the two weeks of camp, he used one of Fergie's stories at campfire each night. He used the reflections and the prayers with each story. Towards the end of camp, a boy of thirteen approached him after campfire, saying, "I think I need to talk to you." This boy had lived through a terrible family tragedy several months earlier, when a close relative had died in a road accident. Since the day of the funeral, the boy had not spoken of the death. The next afternoon, he sat with my colleague for three hours and poured out his heart. He asked difficult questions: What is it like to die? Why is life so unfair? Why did God take my cousin? Can you guarantee that dead people go to heaven? He shared his feelings in words and tears. The story called *Fergie Loses a Friend* broke through the barrier of this boy's grief. Although his questions were hard to answer, asking them brought this boy some peace and comfort that afternoon.

What can you do if a child's question has no certain answer? What if the Church's teaching is too complex for a child to understand yet? What if you don't know what you think about that topic yourself? The third part of this book suggests some resources to help parents and leaders think through basic teachings about faith. First, however, consider the following strategies. Part of the intention with these resources is to have good conversations with children, trusting that God's Spirit moves with us when we seek to know more of God. Having a ready answer is not required for God to be at work within and among us.

When there are many paths to choose from

The examples in this chapter already demonstrate that children ask good questions that have no clear answer, either in the Bible or in the teachings of Christian tradition. Questions about heaven, for example, always lead us to a point where we have to trust God for what we cannot see or know for sure. Sometimes contemporary culture poses situations that are not easily compared with ancient times in our struggle to be faithful. So, if a child's question has no certain answer, at least as you understand Christian faith, you can respond in several ways:

1. Find out the answer that the child proposes first. There is a story behind that question. The child may really seek an opportunity to tell a story or put forward his or her own ideas.
2. Send up a couple of "trial balloons" from your own wondering – perhaps what you thought about that question when you were a child, if you remember, and what you've wondered about it over the years.
3. Interview others – everyone in your family or in your class – to invite their opinions.
4. Let the question remain a question. "Let's think about that for a while. We can talk about it again tomorrow." Maybe the Spirit will inspire some clarity in the interval. Maybe the question won't seem so important in a day or two.

I think the key here lies in respecting a serious question as worth asking and in modelling the truth that not every question will have an easy or quick answer.

When the path ahead is too steep

My formal training in the Church's teaching took more than ten years. I taught in theological college for nine years. Let me say that much of the Church's teaching is difficult for people thoroughly trained in theology to understand and explain. Part of the difficulty arises because we must grapple with ideas shaped in cultures, generations and languages with which we are unfamiliar. Few of us have had the time or inclination to study doctrine beyond what we may learn in a short study course. Yet children wonder about things that truly touch the roots of Christian thinking. Sometimes their questions come from what they hear or see at church. Sometimes their own feelings or logic propose a question that has challenged philosophers for centuries!

The doctrine of the Trinity is an example of a complex teaching in Christian tradition that many theologians struggle to express clearly and understand deeply. Too often it is oversimplified for children using analogies that are not theologically or educationally helpful, like thinking about God as "water, steam and ice." The mystery of God known in Father, Son and Holy Spirit cannot be expressed in a physical comparison like this. Young children will simply be confused. But there are ways – often through art or music – to introduce children to a part of Christian tradition that they can claim.

To stay with the example of the Trinity, I observed in Scotland that children from many different backgrounds and cultures are fascinated by Celtic art. Celtic Christian symbols use geometric designs and unending strands weaving in and out to portray God's unending love and constant presence. Children I worked with loved to draw, trace, paint and colour in Celtic patterns. Because Celtic Christian tradition is so thoroughly Trinitarian, there are many geometrical symbols that work visually with "three in one." Let children identify for themselves how three and one are represented in such symbols. For young children, seeing "three in one" and "one in three" plants the seed of the Church's teaching. There will be time in later years to explore bigger Trinitarian questions!

When the teaching of the Church is too complex for a child to understand, here are a few ways to approach the issue:

1. Look for a theme in that teaching that can be related to a child's life, something you want them to believe even though it doesn't say everything about the topic. I look for a connection that children can grasp, one that will still have integrity when children have grown. The index naming faith themes will help you learn to do this.

2. Look for a hymn or song that you sing in church on that theme, one that uses word pictures rather than concepts in its poetry. Singing the faith even when we can't explain it helps us remember that faith reaches deeper than our understanding. Most hymn books have thorough indexes that can help you trace a theme or a doctrine in different ways.

3. Find a book on Christian art and look for three or four ways in which different artists have expressed a certain theme. Choose art from different centuries and different cultures to open up the wonder in a complex idea. Art doesn't need to be explained. Its power moves us to deeper reflection.

When you don't know where to go

When I work with groups of children, I often find that they test me with questions. The impish children will ask what they think is a shocking question, waiting to see how I respond. I always try to honour questions, even questions put as a dare to provoke me. A question really is an important invitation for both you and the children concerned to grow with God together. If you get stumped by a difficult or daring question, or if you are not really sure what you believe about a topic, welcome to the journey! Don't bluff. Don't deflect the question. This is the moment when we must take Jesus' words very seriously: Ask and it will be given. The biblical text doesn't really specify what "it" is! So trust that exploring the question faithfully is enough, even if a satisfying answer doesn't emerge quickly.

When you are unsure or really puzzled by a question, here are some ways to proceed:

1. Admit that you are not sure. Ask for some time to explore that question. Keep your word by looking for resources that can help. Many churches have libraries with dictionaries and books that offer brief and clear introductions to important themes of the faith.

2. Check your public library and the Internet, too. Of course, not every book or every web site is accurate, so do consult more than one. If you live near a theological college, you may also find a librarian or professor who can help you. Don't be afraid to call.

3. Check with your minister or a church educator. What would they recommend as a simple but sound approach? Not all ministers and priests may know how to translate a complex idea into terms simple enough for young children; staff trained in education will likely be more helpful. But leaders with advanced training in theology can often get you started on your own search. You may have a conversation that helps you sort things out for yourself. Then you'll be better able to talk with your children.

If the child who asks the question is old enough, let her or him join the search with you. If you are working with a group of children, see if a resource person can visit with the whole group. If your children are adept at computer technology, work alongside each other to comb the World Wide Web for information. Show children the kinds of resources you found helpful and teach them how to find such resources. Model ways in which to investigate a good question. If it is a good question, it won't go away while you explore it! Trust that God will honour your search – eventually.

Chapter 3

Patchwork Prayers: Piecing Together Life with God

I learned to pray when I was about three. Like many children, I learned to pray at bedtime, kneeling beside my bed after one of my parents had read me a bedtime story. Together we recited memorized words that began "Now I lay me down to sleep…." After requesting blessing for various family members, friends, neighbours and pets, I would climb back into bed and lay myself down to sleep. This ritual had a nightly rhythm until I was about six. Once I began to read my own bedtime stories, I would call one of my parents to the door of my room for our goodnight prayer. Gradually, I stopped calling. I began to turn out the light by myself. However, I kept up the rhythm of praying at bedtime, beginning with the words that had become so familiar.

It was a very good thing that I didn't give up praying.

The fall I turned eight, I made my annual visit to the optometrist. The doctor spoke to me very seriously after my checkup. He told me that if my eyes kept changing so quickly, I could be blind by the time I was twenty. At least this is how I remember that moment. Whatever else was said, surely that remark was enough to terrify me. At church, I had learned Bible stories about Jesus healing blind people. So in my nightly prayers, I began to urge God to heal my eyes. Every morning I opened my eyes, hoping that the fuzziness would be gone. Every morning I had to grope for my glasses, disappointed. But I never gave up praying.

When I was about ten, I remember waking one day, dreading the daylight, grumbling to God. In that instant, I knew that I was praying the wrong prayer. In that moment, I was given a new prayer. "O God, give me strength to face whatever this day brings." That remains my prayer, spoken or unspoken, as every day begins. The power of that day has carried me through a lot of other blurry days ever since. Yet I never told anyone about it – not my parents, not my sister, certainly not my minister. I did not share the power of that moment until that Sunday after church when five-year-old Beth held out her finger and asked me why God hadn't made her cat scratch go away. The story that began this book began my deeper interest in the spiritual needs of children. My own childhood struggle gave me a place to begin to help Beth face her days with a new prayer.

Prayer has been referred to as the quiet readiness to be addressed. My own childhood experience reinforces this understanding. I trusted that God was always ready to be addressed with my prayers, night after night. But I was not expecting to be addressed *by* God until that startling moment. My memorable childhood encounter with God in prayer continues to shape my hope for children when we teach them to pray. God will engage them in surprising ways as they tell their stories to God in prayer. This sense of prayer as a conversation, when we address God and God in turn addresses us, invites both children and adults to consider prayer as faithful friendship with God.

My image for this chapter comes from quilting, a traditional craft that passes on warmth and comfort from generation to generation. My mother used to call the quilt on my bed a "comforter." I have always connected this quilt with Jesus' promise in the Gospel of John to send us a "comforter" in the Holy Spirit, as the King James Version of the Bible reads. The Holy Spirit prays in us, "with sighs too deep for words," says St. Paul. When we pray with children and encourage them to pray, we take up this gift of God's comforter. My experience praying as a child taught me that God honours the prayers of children, even when we aren't sure what words to use. In this chapter, we will look at when and why children pray and why prayer is important to them as they piece together their place in God's world. Then we'll listen to what children pray about, the fabric of the stories and concerns they offer to God. Next, we'll consider different ways children can pray by looking at the designs for prayer used in Christian worship in many traditions. Finally, we'll explore how families can draw closer together using prayer at home. Each of these themes has its own section:

— Praying Piece by Piece
— The Fabric of Childhood Prayers
— Designs for Our Praying
— Stitched Together in the Spirit

The first two sections focus on comments and prayers from children. The last two sections offer insights from parents and from my experience working with children in worship and small groups.

Praying Piece by Piece

A six-year-old boy, Chris, described prayer as "sort of like a whole bunch of words going together in a rhyme." Many young children in *The Story Project* knew some prayer learned at home by heart, perhaps a grace said before meals or a bedtime prayer. Such prayers are often the foundation for a child's prayer life. As children learn to pray, they can and do pray about other things that concern them. Prayer helps them engage the presence of God in the midst of whatever stirs their souls. That stirring is often invisible to adults around them. In my interviews for *The Story Project*, I asked children about their praying, when they prayed and what they prayed about. Their responses give us a privileged look at some private thoughts and tender moments as children open pieces of life to God and to us.

Lorne, an eight-year-old participant, was quite happy to discuss prayer. He indicated that he likes to say grace at meals, especially when company comes over. His mother's approach to prayer has influenced her son. She has always encouraged him to pray about things that happened each day. Lorne told me that he prays at school, when he's worried about something or when he has trouble getting along with someone. "Please, God, help me get along in school," was the example he gave. His mother smiled at this, for she too had prayed at school as a child. Lorne also noted that he prayed about their house, reflecting a child's concern after hearing about a tragic fire in town. He added that he prayed whenever he was scared or upset, because he felt "very close to God" when he prayed. Linda, at eleven, prayed "to keep my family safe, and when my friends are sick." Linda added that she feels close to God when she's sick "because I have more time to think about him." Speaking to God is an act of trust that God is always near, listening to our stories and concerns. This trust *is* faith.

Many children find prayer a comfort in the midst of scary realities. Tom, at age five, discussed being afraid of the dark with one of my students. Asked whether he called out to his parents when he was afraid, he said, "No, but I talk to God. We have a little chat alone. But I keep my eyes closed…well, sometimes open." Amy, age eight, added a little more to her view of prayer. She suggested that a good time to pray was "when you had to be brave," for example, "when you were going to tell the truth to somebody when you did something wrong." Amy's mother recalled a time when Amy was five. After seeing a news story about a child who was hurt, Amy was quite agitated. Later her mother overheard Amy saying a prayer for the child. Praying seemed to relieve Amy's agitation.

As *The Story Project* progressed in one home, Eric, age eight, began to make up his prayers in his own words. He prayed for his grandparents when they were sick and about things he saw on television. After telling me this, his mother mentioned that she, too, had begun to pray in a new way during the project. As the stories she read with her son stirred up stories in her own heart, she found the courage to pray about sad things in her own life for the first time. In the examples so far, we see just how important praying on their own in their own words is for children. Whether those prayers are spoken in an adult's hearing or rise silently within the child, children's prayers draw them close to God. Parents can develop children's confidence to pray in their own words about things that matter deeply by adding a few spontaneous thoughts about the day after a familiar mealtime grace or bedtime prayer has been repeated. If you are not used to praying aloud in your own words, trust that God will receive with gladness whatever phrase or two you say. Praying in our own words, silently or aloud, feels more natural the more often we open our thoughts to God.

Regular prayer as part of family life encourages children to pray on their own. Yet this may not happen automatically. The children in one family reported to me that "we pray mainly at church, at bedtime, and before dinner." These sisters explained that breakfast time was "just too busy" for praying at their house. When they discussed a story about Sherman in which everything seems to go wrong, both girls told their mother that they didn't think about praying when they had a bad day. "This is surprising," their mother reflected. "We have been praying with the children since they were very young, yet still they don't think to pray when things go wrong." A few nights later, however, her older daughter prayed aloud at bedtime "that Mummy have a better day tomorrow." The mother smiled to herself, recognizing that she had been angry that day. "I am pretty sure my daughter has prayed this way before. Perhaps she just wasn't naming how she prays."

This mother's insight is helpful, for prayer is not an easy topic for conversation in many families. It is deeply personal for children as well as adults. Her daughter later commented to me, "Prayer is important to God, and I think it's important, too." Prayerful friendship with God is nourished bit by bit when families pray together at various times and in different ways. It is also supported in little conversations that address the daily ups and downs of family life. If a child primarily offers prayers that make requests of God, a chance to talk about those requests is helpful. When a child is disappointed that such a request goes "unanswered," parent and child can talk about other ways to approach God on that topic – and other ways to look at the situation that stimulated the child's request.

His mother noticed that five-year-old Kent had started to pray on his own after bedtime prayer ended and his parents left his room. The subject of his prayers was Rascal, a cat who had disappeared. "He tells God that Rascal is missing and asks that God help Rascal find his way home." In my interview I asked Kent about Rascal. Kent told me at first he prayed that God would bring Rascal back home. Then Kent admitted it had been a few weeks now and that he didn't think Rascal was coming home. "So now I pray that God will help Rascal find a good home wherever he is." Kent's mother was sure his prayers helped him work through his feelings about Rascal. I appreciate the ways in which Kent continues to tell his story to God, chapter by chapter, week by week. He trusts that God is listening even though his first request didn't come to pass.

Anna, age nine, developed this theme a little further. She remembered praying for her father when he was sick. She was very happy that he got better. Then she added, "But if you pray for new blue jeans, your mom and dad have to buy the jeans anyway." Her insight suggests an understanding of prayer that moves beyond the fulfillment of human wishes. Prayer is different than presenting a list of desires to Santa Claus. Thinking of faith as trust in God and prayer as a conversation with God who is always listening shifts our concerns about whether prayer is "answered." A conversation is more than questions and answers. A six-year-old girl put it well when she said to me, "We are friends with God when we pray."

These examples show us that children consider prayer quite deeply. It is an important piece of their faith in God. They pray for many reasons, at different times and places. Let us look more closely at the concerns children place before God.

The Fabric of Childhood Prayers

There is at least one story woven into every prayer we offer. When Beth presented me with her tiny cat scratch, I recognized many stories shaping her question of why it was still there. She began with the story of her new kitten, whose claws had left that small mark on her finger. There was also the story of Beth's request to God, tested carefully each day for results. But in Beth's life there were many other stories of trips to the doctor, daily insulin injections, and both family and medical attention focused on a young diabetic. Each of these stories needed a listening ear: a parent's, a pastor's or God's.

After my conversation with Beth, I began to think more carefully about the prayers that accompany the stories I tell. I want those prayers to encourage children to tell God what is happening in their lives. Whether by writing a prayer in advance or praying aloud spontaneously, I try to form prayers that are conversational in tone, rather than a list of requests. I choose words that children themselves use. My instinct is to let prayers express to God the feelings a story stirs up. Then, when life stirs up such feelings again, we have heard at least one prayer that helps us seek God when our feelings are bubbling inside. Whether our feelings are happy or sad, whether they arise from conflict or celebration or uncertainty, we can present them to God. Feelings form the fabric of many prayers in this collection. Over the years, this model of praying with children has invited some remarkable responses.

A teacher who uses stories about Fergie the Frog with her classes in a Roman Catholic elementary school sent me some prayers that her students had written as they worked with my stories. I was deeply touched by the range of concerns that these eight- and nine-year-olds presented to God. Many of their prayers say thanks to God for families, for pets, for food and for good times enjoyed that day. "Dear God, Thank you for all your creations, animals, plants, trees and water. Rain, food and sunshine. Thank you for my life and the world I live in," wrote one boy. His prayer reflects a child's great sense of connection with the world around. I see the same concern at work in the children's prayers for other people. "Please help the homeless and the poor," prayed a young girl. "Give them strength to go on with their lives without sorrow and bring laughter to all of the children who are poor." Prayer is a natural time to express compassion for others, compassion that children feel deeply. In their classroom prayers, these children prayed for the sick, for people facing floods and hurricanes, for peace in the world and for God to keep newborn babies "healthy and clean." In such prayers, children offer up glimpses of stories that are important to them from their families and from the world around them.

This small collection of prayers also provided a window into pieces of the children's personal lives. "Dear, Lord, I feel so alone. I need your help to find strength. My friends have moved away," wrote another girl. In a similar tone, a boy prayed, "God, I'm talking to you because I'm lonely. Can you help me find someone to play with?" "Dear Lord, something terrible has happened in my life," confessed another child. "I need the courage to go on." The stories woven into the fabric of these prayers are known to God's heart alone. How precious is the trust in God that these children express as they open up their own hearts.

Another common theme in these prayers is request for guidance. "Dear God, help us to make good decisions.... Help us not to be careless when we make our decisions." "Please watch upon us so we don't get scared." "Help us to tell someone when we are angry and lonely." All these phrases come from three- or four-sentence prayers voiced by children themselves. They remind us that children in school face many challenges. How important it is to connect daily challenges to God, who is always with us. As one girl put it, "I just feel like talking to you, God, because I enjoy talking to you and I love you." With this kind of confidence in God's listening ear, children can develop a prayerful friendship with God, for good times as well as times of distress.

During my summer in Scotland, I received a wonderful gift from a six-year-old girl. We had read several stories and prayers from this collection the week she visited. After our last evening session ended, she waited for me by herself. Then she handed me a sheet of paper torn from a notebook. It was folded and folded and folded again. Inside, in silver ink, she offered these prayers (with names changed but not her spelling!):

— dear god, thank you for the sun and the moon and the stars. The world looks beautiful with little hairy and big creatures of the world. Amen.

— dear god, Please save people from dieing and thank for being by are side. Thank you for my goldfish who's called Rodger and for Mairi's hamster and Megan's goldfish. Amen.

— dear god, Please please don't bring death for daddy's cats and his rabbit and Fiona's rabbit and their kitten. Please don't make me forget my friends and my old teacthers. Amen.

Her page is illustrated with sun, moon, stars and a friendly bunch of hamsters, cats and goldfish. It is a genuine and surprising expression of her concern. Her prayers are also interesting because they express in turn what Christian tradition calls *thanksgiving*, *praise*, *intercession* and *supplication*. Although she would not know these terms yet, her life in Christian community has given her many different designs for her prayers. It is worth considering how children can use different ways of praying to draw near to God at different times in their lives.

Designs for Our Praying

Many children learn a mealtime grace or a bedtime prayer that becomes the foundation of their praying. The words I learned as a child years ago are still familiar to children I meet:

Now I lay me down to sleep
I pray the Lord my soul to keep.
If I should die before I wake,
I pray the Lord my soul to take.

In my childhood ritual, this prayer was followed by the phrase "God bless...." Then I prayed aloud a list of people and pets in need of blessing. In *Story Project* interviews, I met several children who had learned this same prayer, or a modified version of it. They, too, offered a list of names for God to bless. "How does God bless people?" I asked Paul, age seven. He shrugged. "I don't know how you bless." *Bless* is one of those words in Christian tradition that is not easy for a young child to grasp. A child can say such words but their meaning is not obvious.

Many adults who learned this old prayer as children now shudder at its rhyme, feeling that its references to dying are too ghoulish for a good night's sleep. That feeling may well be justified, given improved life expectancy for children in many parts of the developed world these days. In its origins, this prayer reflected the faithful struggle of generations who faced high rates of infant mortality, trusting to God children who died too soon. The text of the prayer contains a few words that very young children don't understand, like the word *soul*. Even the implications of dying are not really clear to many children. Though these words may disguise the prayer's request to some degree, its tone remains rather distant. You can find new versions of this prayer that change the last two lines into a more peaceful rhyme, drawing the child closer to God for a good night's sleep.

This prayer shows us the challenge in choosing language to teach children to pray. We search for words that speak of feelings and experience in ways children recognize. If a prayer you are learning contains an unusual word for children, offer an example they'll know from experience. To *bless* someone is to be kind to that person, to bring good things into someone's life. So God can bless us and we can bless each other. We bless God by telling the world about God's goodness. Children will be able to say how people are blessed once they connect the word to their own experience of kind acts and good things. *Soul* is much harder to compare to something familiar. Philosophers have debated its meaning for centuries. To a child, I might say that my soul is what makes me a special person and your soul makes you a special person too. God loves us, body and soul, for we are special to God, each in our own way.

Learning a prayer by heart is one way children start to pray. However, a memorized prayer will not always say what is on a child's mind. Christian worship teaches us to express different human needs before God in different ways. Think about a worship service that you've attended. Whatever tradition is familiar to you, you have likely participated in several different kinds of prayer during worship. Prayers offer to God different human responses: praise, confession, thanks and request are very common forms of public prayer. We pray in different ways during worship, too. Sometimes we read a prayer together. Sometimes we pray spontaneously about today's concerns. Prayer can be silent listening – to God or to the words of a worship leader. Some prayers we recite are common to all Christians. Others are familiar to a particular tradition or local church. In worship, children can learn how to reach out to God in different ways – especially if we help children make the language of our prayer traditions their own. In the following sections, I rephrase traditional language for prayers used in worship as simple statements a child can make. These phrases may help you translate the voices of our Christian heritage into a child's vocabulary and daily life. I also offer some ideas about concrete ways to live out our prayers together.

Praying our praise – God, we love you! You are amazing!

Worship services often begin with singing and speaking prayers of praise. We declare how great is God, our Maker. In praise, we wonder aloud at the beauty of the world and God's precious gift of life. "Praise" is a word that young children will not understand readily, however. It is something we give and receive usually without using that word. We can help a child learn what praise is when we take time to praise God in small moments of wonder. Offer a simple line of praise in plain language when you stand with a child and watch an interesting bug crawl across a leaf or when you count the stars on a clear night: "God, even the bugs in your world are amazing!" "God, your stars are so beautiful, they take my breath away." Say it out loud. Don't worry what your neighbours think! In such a simple way, a child's proclaiming of God's greatness begins.

There are sentences from many psalms that can help children offer prayers of praise, as they learn to recognize the word *praise*. Use the words in Psalm 148 to help a child imagine how different creatures "sing" praise to God. Or repeat the opening verse of Psalm 47 together, clapping your hands for God in praise. "Alleluia" is a word of praise that echoes through generations of God's people. Children can learn to sing settings of this word as it is used in worship. Those songs can become choruses of praise used in a moment of wonder or happiness. A story featuring Sherman the Hound Dog helps children talk about different ways we can praise God. In *Fetch*, Sherman is praised in different ways as he learns something new. When we talk about this story, I ask the children to name different ways that we can tell God of our love in worship or show God our love day by day. This story tries to connect words of praise with acts of praise offered to God.

Saying grace – We thank you, God!

Children are often taught to say "please" and "thank you" as soon as they begin to change sounds of request into words. The importance of saying thank you to each other grows from our thanks to God. When we worship, we say thanks to God for the gift of life itself and for the ways in which creatures make life good and livable for each other. *Grace* means gift, one freely given. Saying grace is saying thanks for what God gives us from the great store of God's love. Build on children's excitement over birthday gifts or Christmas presents to help them see that God gives us many wonders day by day. We can say or sing our thanks in prayer on ordinary days, too.

Saying grace at meals acknowledges that the food we eat is a gift of God's creation, even though we pay for it and prepare it for our table. Our thanks at mealtime could extend to thanks for the hands that grow and carry our food to market, all God's helpers in the cycle of living that feeds us. We can also show our thanks in giving gifts to others in need of food. Praying our thanks leads to living out our thanks after we leave the meal table by sharing what we can with the hungry. This thankful stance is not easy to take in a society where "we get what we pay for." We encourage children to grow up as grateful and generous people when they see gratitude expressed and generosity shared among the people who are closest to them.

As children grow and begin to study how the world works, they soon become aware that we eat animals whose lives are taken for human benefit. Sometimes children's sensitivity to this leads to requests for vegetarian meals. I know many vegetarians whose commitment to their diet began when they were eight or nine years old. In many Aboriginal traditions, taking life from plants and animals to nourish human life is named and honoured in prayer. Such prayer recognizes that we are all connected to each other by our Maker and that human beings have special responsibility to honour the rest of creation that provides our food. If the food chain becomes an issue of faithfulness in your family, take the opportunity to talk together about the many connections between all God's creatures. Work out a way of consuming that respects the give and take between creatures and tries not to consume more than a fair share.

Saying thanks at the end of the day extends thanksgiving to other "gifts" life brings. A bedtime story can open up stories from the day, suggesting important people and events as the focus of our thanks to God. Many of the stories in this collection highlight one aspect of our thanks that day – for friends, for family, for what we learn, etc. A mother commented in our interview, "I suddenly realized that I have never taught the kids to pray when they are thankful or happy." Mostly she had prayed with her children for God's healing and guidance. We can also give God thanks when we have made it through a difficult time or made up after a disagreement. Our thanks to God are not only related to *what* we receive, but also *who* is connected to us and *what happens* around us.

Saying "the grace"

The traditional Trinitarian benediction "The grace of our Lord Jesus Christ, the love of God and the communion of the Holy Spirit" is often referred to as "the grace." Sometimes a priest or minister pronounces these words as a blessing at the end of worship. Sometimes Christians bless each other with "the grace," saying the words aloud together. Children can learn to say this ancient blessing for those times and places where we call God's blessing on our whole family or community. Remember that its phrasing can be confusing to a child. A child will likely associate "grace" directly with a mealtime prayer, not with the gift of mercy and new life we receive through Jesus Christ. "Communion" will remind children of the celebrations with bread and wine they observe or share in at church. The larger meaning of our unity in the Spirit and the community of fellowship we share as the Church will not be familiar to young children. If you want to teach your children to say "the grace," take some time to explore each phrase with them. You can look for stories on God's love and forgiveness using the thematic index in Part III. Stories on these important themes bring the meaning of each phrase to life from a child's perspective.

Confessing in prayer – God, see what has happened!

Presbyterian worship has traditionally included a public prayer to confess our sin to God, sometimes at great length. Other Christian traditions use somewhat different models for confession in their liturgies, combining private and public expressions of "things done and left undone." Over the years, I have heard people of various backgrounds complain about prayers of confession. They feel that such prayers are "too negative" and reflect an "old-fashioned" emphasis on sin. However, in Chapter 2, comments from children reveal that they know when life is not unfolding as it should. They feel let down by friends. They find it hard to share with each other. They nod knowingly when a story tells of lies, temper tantrums or broken rules. Perhaps we should understand *confession* as pouring our hearts out to God anytime things don't feel right. Sometimes we confess what we have done on our own, when we realize that our actions have hurt somebody or something. Sometimes we confess what has been done to us and how that makes us feel. Sometimes we confess what is going wrong in the world around us and the part we play together in the midst of this muddle. In confession we say to God, "See what has happened."

Many times, a character in my stories must face the unhappy consequences of action, whether intended or unintended. When praying with children about these times, when "confessing sins," it is vital to claim God's forgiveness. *Forgiveness* in Christian perspective is not escape from unhappy consequences. It is a God-given opportunity to learn a new way of relating or responding to one another. The promise of the Gospel is that God will not turn away from us, even when we "sin" and hurt God or God's world. God comes to us to help us clean up our lives and try a new way. Often the prayers in this book include a prayer for God's help to try again or to set things right with each other. Prayers of confession joined with prayers for God's support are an important source of strength to try this new way.

When someone has hurt us, a prayer of confession may also be appropriate. Pain and anger may be just as much part of our confessing to God as are shame or regret. A child who has felt embarrassed or rejected through the actions of someone else can learn to trust those feelings to God. It is not easy to deal with embarrassment or rejection at school or among playmates. Confessing how we feel when we've been hurt can be the first step in healing. It can also manage the urge to strike back in anger and revenge. Talking about such disappointments with each other is important. Teaching children to pray when others hurt them gives them faithful resources to seek God's strength when there is no one else to talk to. When we release troubled feelings and situations to God, God helps us to make a fresh start.

As well as praying for ourselves when someone has hurt us, we need to be able to pray for those who have hurt us, for our "enemies," to use Jesus' words in Matthew 5.43-44. In Christian faith, the cycle of confession and forgiveness leads to reconciliation. These big words won't make much sense to young children, yet children feel the strain when someone who was a friend is no longer friendly. They can learn to make or remake a friendship by treating someone as they would like to be treated. But living out this Golden Rule (Matthew 7.12) takes courage and trust in the hidden working of the Spirit of God. Praying for someone we're mad at, for someone who has hurt us, invites God to work for change in the whole situation, not just in our own hearts.

Asking God about our lives – God, help us!

"God bless Mommy and Daddy and Uncle George and Aunt Jane and Freddie and Sean and Susan and Gloria and my teacher and Mr. Jones. Oh, and Grandma and Grandpa, too." Many childhood prayers celebrate long lists of loving, shared equitably among family, friends, Freddie the family dog and Gloria the goldfish. When we pray for others, we often have a request in mind. We want something or someone in our world to get better. Christian tradition calls these prayers, where we ask God to act in a situation, *petitions* or *intercessions*. Prayers about the details of living are a deeply significant part of faith. They also raise deeply significant questions about God's ways in the world, questions that are sometimes hard to answer.

Marjorie Suchocki's study on prayer, *In God's Presence*, provides a helpful way to think about praying for the well-being of others. God has shared God's power with all creation. Otherwise, we creatures would not have the strength and abilities we do. In a world where God shares power, God works with the world "as it is," responding with us to situations in which we play a role. Suchocki reminds us that "God may use us in answer to our prayers."[12] Often, however, we pray as if God alone had all the power and all the responsibility for our lives, at least when things go wrong. Then, when requests are not "answered" in the time or ways we desire, God alone bears the blame. Many broken hearts remain unhealed when God is blamed for "unanswered prayer" over a lifetime.

My five-year-old cat scratch victim already knew the pang of such prayer. We need to guide children when they pray with specific requests in mind. When I asked Beth if the scratch was getting better, she quickly agreed that you could hardly see it anymore. I proposed to her that God made our bodies so some things like a little scratch got better on their own, day by day. Beth nodded and added, "If you keep it clean like Mommy said." I also pictured the work of doctors and nurses as another way that God takes care of our bodies when other things go wrong. I wanted Beth to think of all the people who cared for her as sharing in God's healing work. Prayer engages God in our world as we know it. At the same time, God engages us to respond to that world as part of God's action.

When we pray for God to act on our concerns, we can also ask God to guide and strengthen us to respond to those situations. Think of a family saying grace during Lent and adding to their thanks for their meal a prayer for hungry people. That prayer for the hungry moves from word into action if the family agrees to set aside some money each week for a hunger project. Or perhaps that family can help serve Easter dinner to the hungry in their own neighbourhood. So, too, when we pray for God to heal and comfort a sick friend, we can ask God to help us see how we can comfort, support and "bless" that person.

Lamenting our sorrow – God, how can this be? Where are you?

Marjorie Suchocki also observes that prayers take place in the midst of the limits to human life. So often, however, we beg God to remove those limits, at least for a while. Helping children recognize that life has limits is part of growing up with God. When those limits bring us face to face with suffering and death, it is important to claim another ancient prayer tradition, *lament*. While young children may express themselves in tears fairly often, as they grow up many receive the message that tears are unacceptable. Instead, in times of tragedy, we should think of tears as our lament to God, who will wipe away our tears whenever sorrow wells up within us (Revelation 7.17; Isaiah 25.8).

In the Bible, lament is a form of storytelling. In the midst of crisis or despair, a story pours forth from the heart. Someone cries out to God, declaring that something is wrong. Feelings of anger and despair are hurled at God, for the speaker often feels betrayed. Yet, once these strong feelings are released to God, lament turns to the story of God's faithfulness. A lament rehearses the times when God has been good. As this part of the story unfolds, a lament climbs from the depth of sorrow towards a new dawn. Lament ends in trust and thanksgiving that God's steadfast love will see us through crisis. If we take this shape of lament as a framework for a child's experience of sorrow, we learn some important features of prayer.

Lament teaches us not to turn away from strong feelings but to voice those feelings to God. God's love is strong enough to receive our anger, sadness and fear. Our own hearts can break if we try to keep those feelings bottled up. If children develop a prayerful friendship with God, a friendship where stories are told and feelings poured out, God will be a child's companion in sad or scary times. Sometimes adults try to silence the searching questions and the sorrow of children. Usually such efforts intend to make things less painful and more manageable for children (and for the adults, too!). But too often a pool of tears and sorrow collects within children as they grow unless they learn to tell tearful stories and cry out for help when they need it. As adults we will need support to face our own grief and loss when children need our help at the same time.

Lament in Scripture also teaches us to tell the whole story. We begin by telling of loss or fear, but then we remember where we have come from, who is with us, and why this experience matters to us. Lament reminds us that we are not alone on our journey through sorrow. We find strength to take a step forward even when the future seems uncertain. In any time of grieving, retelling the good and glad memories that we will always treasure is another source of strength. A child's journey through lament could be expressed through drawing. Through pictures and colours, a child can express a prayer of sadness, remember special times as a prayer of thanks, and imagine a scene of hope set in the future. Artwork can be both a prayerful and a pastoral action for children, offered to God and perhaps to others who will find a child's drawings expressive of their own heartfelt stories.

Our Father...

The Lord's Prayer is another piece of Christian tradition that children need to learn if they are to be part of the Church. Lisa's declaration in Chapter 2 that "the kangaroos are coming" points out that this prayer is not easy for small children to understand. It is not easy to remember, either, because it lacks an easy rhythm for the tongue. Learning the words with a musical setting or some actions will help. Young children will gradually absorb those words until they become an unforgettable pattern of speech. As children learn to read on their own, make a bookmark or poster with the words to the Lord's Prayer for them. There are several different versions of The Lord's Prayer now in common use. Help your children learn by heart the one that your congregation uses most frequently. Older children will be interested to know why different versions exist and will want to talk about what the differences mean.

I learned a set of body movements for The Lord's Prayer when I spent a summer on the Isle of Iona. A leader in the adult program taught us gestures that express the words symbolically. We later taught these gestures to our group of children. One evening, as we led the children on a tour of the Iona abbey, I suggested that we say the "family prayer" of all Christians in that wondrous space, using the movements we'd learned. First we did so, saying the words aloud. Then a seven-year-old girl piped up. "Can we pray it just using the actions?" So we prayed in silence, with our bodies "speaking." The moment was filled with reverence. At the end of the week, when the children drew their favourite memories of their holiday, this girl drew herself, arms lifted towards the sky. "It's me, doing the Lord's Prayer in silence in the abbey." Remembering is not just a task of the mind. Using our bodies to move with words roots those words deeply within us.

"Who is this God guy, anyway?" A four-year-old boy asked his mother this question during a worship service I led. He did not attend church regularly. His comment points to a concern for many adults when children hear the language of Christian tradition. Is God "a guy"? Do Jesus' words "Our Father" mean that God is male in the same way human men are male? In this generation, the names we choose to address God have become a source of controversy among believers. It is beyond the scope of this book to explore current discussion about the names we use to address God. However, I want to highlight a few points to consider when talking and praying with children.

Naming God in prayer calls on us to borrow language from our lives, from our world and from Christian tradition to speak of what we know – and of what we do not yet fully know. The names we use regularly in prayer have a powerful impact on a child's sense of who God is in their lives. In many Christian churches from different historical traditions, language for God found in hymns and prayers has been changing. New and less familiar word pictures open up our understanding of God for fresh reflection. God is "named" as mother and rock and eagle, as well as father and king and light. All these images can be found in Scripture, yet some of them are much more familiar to us than others.

In the prayers written by children described earlier in this chapter, the children used "God" or "Lord" to begin their prayers most often. These terms reflect what they hear regularly in worship. We want our children to learn the names for God commonly used in the church we attend. In prayer, we want to approach God with names that can be both personal and at the same time reverent. Whatever words we use to address God, we must recognize that God is more mysterious and surprising than any single name suggests. Using a few different names for God to begin prayer helps a child recognize the mystery of God before that child understands what a mystery is.

The Bible offers many word pictures of God's action in our lives. In Psalm 131, God is pictured as a mother holding a child on her breast. Jesus describes his ministry as a hen gathering chicks in Luke 13.34. The work of the Spirit is seen as the wind blowing in John 3. New hymns and prayers for worship now play with many of these traditional yet uncommon images. In a fairly new Canadian hymn book, I found these three Scripture texts reflected in poetic phrases from three different hymns: Mothering God, Sheltering God, and Wind of God. Such phrases are pleasing to an adult's ear but they can confuse a young child who is not yet able to use symbols in this way. "Mothering" is an abstract idea for a child still learning to say or spell "mother." Such word pictures can be turned into longer phrases that have a clearer connection to life as a child knows it:

God, when we feel lonely, you cuddle us like a mother cuddles her baby.

Jesus, when we're afraid, protect us like a hen who gathers her chicks under her wings.

God, you move around us like the wind; give us life like a breath of fresh air.

Turning creative but unfamiliar names for God into a sentence describing God's action will be more helpful for younger children. By the time children are eight or nine, however, they can begin to explore images and symbols as creative ways of addressing God.

The prayers in this collection most often open with the simple name "God" or the phrase "Dear God." Sometimes I address a prayer to Jesus, usually when a story's theme comes from a particular story about Jesus that I want children to recall. When we are beginning to teach children to pray, a simple and familiar opening like "Dear God" is less confusing than a metaphor. As the child grows and develops new cognitive abilities, new names and images for God can help a familiar practice of prayer flower once it has taken root.

Praying the songs of our souls

In Christian worship, every kind of prayer described here is sung as often as it is spoken. Sometimes the words of a hymn or song offer prayer. Sometimes churches chant brief prayers at different points in their liturgies. Music embodies the rhymes and reasons of our relationship with God differently than words alone. Using musical settings of prayers from your local church service to pray at home is a good way to help children learn to participate in worship. Is there a song of praise or thanksgiving used when the offering is taken? Perhaps this song could be used as a mealtime prayer from time to time. If your congregation sings responsive phrases during prayer or uses short songs for certain parts of the service, teach your children to sing these songs as prayers. Hum them at bedtime or when you're out for a walk. An "Alleluia" sung when the Gospel lesson is read can be a prayer of praise to God in the backyard, too. *Kyrie eleison*, which means "Lord, have mercy," is an ancient prayer sung to many different melodies. Sing it to each other when it's time to say "sorry" and start again.

Music is central to spiritual life for both old and young. Sometimes adults think that children enjoy only short, simple tunes with snappy rhythms and maybe some handclapping to accompany the words. Of course, such songs do express a child's praise of God with joy and energy. But several children I interviewed on the Isle of Iona spoke of the "gentle songs" and the "quiet services" as moments when they felt especially welcome in worship. Children also have an ear for the haunting cadences of Gregorian chant and Celtic folk tunes. Melodies from Aboriginal and Asian cultures move in mysterious ways that invite children to wonder about God and the world. Music from churches all over the world now finds a place in hymn books and worship services far from its home base. The children I worked with in Scotland loved to sing these songs, moving with the rhythms of places they'd never been. An eight-year-old girl said, "I like singing those funny songs that I don't know what they mean but I can sing them." Her words remind us that prayer and praise take us beyond what we understand. Music draws us towards God with heart, body, mind and soul awakened to the Spirit. Children are often more ready than adults to enjoy worship and prayer that move us in such tangible ways.

Stitched Together in the Spirit

Prayer is not always an easy topic for a family to engage. Different traditions and beliefs that have shaped parents' views can complicate ideas about how to pray with children. So, too, with many activities pulling family members in different directions on their own timetables, making space and time for family prayer is a challenge. Yet children need to observe the practice of prayer within a busy home in order to learn to pray. One mother in the project had enrolled her daughter in a Christian after-school program. She commented:

> My experience growing up was that prayer was a private matter. I had assumed the same thing for Claire. I didn't realize until she joined this program that Claire didn't have an inkling about what prayer is.

The model proposed in this book provides one way to start praying about things that happen to many of us as children. Each story takes from five to seven minutes to read aloud. Using the short reflection and prayer that follow adds another minute or two. Without any further discussion, listeners focus attention on our lives as God's children for about ten minutes. Several families who participated in *The Story Project* used this model to start a family pattern for daily prayer. The parents of twins were grateful for the invitation to begin:

> The boys like the idea of prayer. They sing grace all the time. We overhear them saying the prayer from children's time at church when they're just wandering around. Now they want to be able to say the prayer after each story along with their dad.

Establishing a daily pattern for prayer when children are quite young is a wise beginning for a family. Even before a child is able to listen to a five-minute story, that child can learn a one-line prayer to use at mealtime or bedtime. Taking just a few seconds to pray at each meal, or even one meal a day, sows the seeds for a child's prayer life. Bookstores usually carry collections of mealtime and bedtime prayers written especially for the young. Rhythm, repetition and rhyme in words appeal to very young ears. The familiar mealtime prayer "God is great. God is good. Let us thank God for our food!" offers rhythm and repeated sounds in its short phrases that help very young children learn it. Children also enjoy the rhythms in Celtic prayer that please the ear when spoken aloud. Collections of such prayers often have the added gift of beautiful illustrations and script that children love to look at.

One *Story Project* family already had the custom to pray before and after their evening meal. They chose to use the stories and prayers after the meal ended, before the children disappeared from the table. The younger boys were always eager to choose the story to be read but were not particularly attentive to the reflections. When I asked the oldest brother, who was nine, about the stories, he said in a serious way, "They help me to think about things a lot." No two children will respond in the same way or at the same time to the power of storytelling or the practice of prayer. Yet the perseverance of these parents to offer a regular pattern for talking about faith trusted that, in their own ways, each of their sons would learn to engage God day by day.

Several families in *The Story Project* read the stories and prayed together but then sought quiet moments following the stories for parent and child to talk out the questions one-on-one. Giving each child special attention adds a sense of personal value within the family and of a special relationship with God. One-on-one time also keeps a parent alert to individual struggles or challenges a child is facing. A bedtime story and prayer provide significant opportunities to reflect with each child on the day just ending. One mother discovered bathtime as a good time for conversation about stories read earlier. In all these ways, the rhythms of storytelling and prayer that a family shares together help each child's faith find expression.

The patience and perseverance to keep setting aside time within family routines for prayer are vital. In the Gospel of Luke, Jesus tells a parable about our need "to pray always and not to lose heart" (Luke 18.1-8). It is easy to lose heart about praying "always," given the many demands in family life. If you start a pattern for family prayer and then discover it has fallen to the wayside, don't despair! Just start again! Perhaps choosing a new time or a new way of praying will inspire your family in a fresh way. If your church celebrates Advent or Lent, these seasons of Christian storytelling offer a great opportunity to begin or begin again to celebrate with the whole Christian community. If candles are part of your prayer tradition, then light a family prayer candle with your meals. A flickering flame focuses our attention on the mysterious movement of God and invites young children to recognize a special moment of holy time. In such small ways, children can find their feet as those who know God and follow God's ways day by day.

If your family struggles a little to find ways of praying that are comfortable and comforting, don't lose heart. Remember what the Letter to the Romans promises: The Spirit helps us in our weakness; for we do not know how to pray as we ought, but that very Spirit intercedes with sighs too deep for words (Romans 8.26).

Perhaps the whole family cannot participate in prayer together. In that case, trust that those who do share prayer from time to time, in quiet corners or quick moments, are heard by God. Their prayers hold the whole family before God. Even our silent thoughts and deep sighs lift our stories before God, no matter what our age. Our thoughts and sighs also address us with God's voice and God's presence. For prayer is "quiet readiness" in which God may speak or move within us. If we grow up trusting that God hears and responds, sometimes in mysterious ways, then the patchwork of our lives will be stitched together by the Spirit, who works with all the pieces of our prayers. Amen. May it be so for you!

Chapter 4

Developing an Appetite for God

"Try it! You might like it!"

These words of encouragement pepper a child's mealtime experience whenever new food offerings appear on the plate. Strange vegetables and suspicious sauces provoke stubborn reactions in many young eaters. Sometimes the thought of introducing prayer and faith conversations into a family's routine or a children's program can trigger similar resistance. We may feel a little awkward or uncertain exploring the language of faith, at least until we know what to expect from each other – and from God.

The model proposed in this collection is rooted in storytelling for good reason. Everyone can listen to a story. Given a chance, most people like to tell a story. These stories sample the familiar flavours of childhood. When a story feels familiar, a short prayer about that story is only a small step to take. As my mother used to say to me in my days as a finicky eater, "Just try one! You might like it." With her gentle encouragement, I gradually developed my taste for vegetables and more exotic recipes. Using the resources in this book with such gentle encouragement can open up the life-giving resources of God for children (and adults) whose appetite for prayer and God-talk is just developing.

There are four parts to this chapter, each of which is designed to consider important aspects of using these resources in different situations. The first section will look once again at ways to use this material at home, considering questions not touched upon in Chapter 3. In the second section, the discussion explores ideas for introducing this model into programs for children – as part of a Christian education curriculum, for example, or with activity groups. Then we examine issues facing storytellers who work with children during worship. Finally, there are some storytelling tips to consider when gathering groups of various sizes to listen to a story in different kinds of spaces. Because I hope these ideas will nourish the faith of children at home and at church, I have chosen food imagery to focus our considerations in all four sections.

— Home Cooking – Tasting Stories with Your Family
— Food for Thought – Stirring Stories into Children's Programs
— Bread for the Journey – Sampling Stories in Worship Settings
— Ingredients for Effective Storytelling

Each section is divided into brief comments that respond to questions and suggestions that parents, grandparents and church leaders raised during *The Story Project*.

Home Cooking – Tasting Stories with Your Family

The family provides the foundation for much of a child's growing life of faith. Research has shown again and again that bedtime and mealtime prayers set up memorable moments for children that can launch their relationships with God. Home is where the heart is, the old saying goes. Home can warm the heart of faith within a child when faith becomes a topic honoured in family conversation and action. The family, whatever shape it takes, is the cradle in which children receive most of the values by which they will live. Both faith in God and faithfulness in human relations are developed through our families to a great extent. I use the words "faith" and "faithfulness" to link what we believe about God with the values that guide us to become trustworthy citizens and generous neighbours. Encouraging children to grow in faith and faithfulness is as important to their future health as cultivating their taste in vegetables!

Parents, grandparents and godparents have a crucial role to play in fostering faithful curiosity and compassion for the world in each new generation of children. The same can be said of those aunts, uncles and adult friends of the whole family. Each significant adult in a child's life contributes to that child's appreciation of God as a life companion when we demonstrate God's significance in what we do and how we live. Let's look at some issues facing families who want to explore this collection of stories as a way to develop conversations about faith and values.

When can we find time to get started?

Setting aside a regular time to listen to one of these stories and talk about it together gradually introduces faith as a regular part of family life. "Regular" could mean reading a story once a day or once a week, depending on your schedule. Chapter 3 describes different ways that families who tested this material got started. Many of them found it a challenge to schedule regular time for a story and prayer, but persistence paid off! For families who gather for a meal together most days, a few minutes before or after the meal to hear a story and share a prayer can add to the value of eating together. Perhaps scheduling a "family meeting" for a story and conversation once a week will be more convenient, especially when children are busy with different activities. With young children, bedtime is another quiet moment for both story and prayer. Whatever pattern you try, give it a chance to settle in to family routines before you evaluate it. Learning to enjoy new experiences can take time, just like developing a taste for a new food does. A comfortable pattern for your family will emerge if you try out different suggestions for a while.

Conversations that arise from stories can fit in around the edges of a day. A couple of parents mentioned significant moments in the car driving to and from other activities when children raised things to discuss. When parent and child undertake some household chore together, an opportunity to talk may present itself. These other activities create a larger framework in which to consider important things. Both parent and child can take a bit of time to think things through while concentrating on the tasks at hand.

Several families in the research project found that it took most of the first month to get used to using this material together. Especially if your family has not talked about faith together very much, it often takes a while to feel comfortable putting ideas and questions about God into your own words. Each story with its reflection and prayer can be read in less than ten minutes. If you decide to talk about a story as a family group, be sure to allow enough time for each person to consider whether they have something to add to the conversation. Some people just naturally take a little longer to say their ideas out loud. If you are leading a family discussion, after a few minutes invite quieter members to add their thoughts. "Would you like to add anything?" is an open-ended way to offer "air time" without putting a quiet person on the spot.

How do we decide which stories to use?

Stories in this collection were written over several years in response to many different influences in children's lives. There is no set place to begin. Most stories stand on their own. The stories have been indexed by the feelings a story explores, the life situation presented and a faith theme connected to that life situation. This index can help you find stories for a particular moment in your family's life. It can be just as fruitful, however, to use stories randomly and listen for issues percolating within your children.

Another way to begin is to choose one character and get to know the model for reflection by following that character's adventures. In the story collection, each character's stories are grouped together. Recall briefly the points made in Chapter 1. Fergie the Frog stories often appeal to younger children, for whom the family is the main social group. Jackie Rabbit and Sherman the Hound Dog introduce themes children face as they begin to act more independently at school and with their friends. The age range of your listeners may suggest which stories to select first.

Children in *The Story Project* sometimes had a favourite character. Certain stories also emerged as ones to be read again and again. Once your children become familiar with these stories, they may enjoy selecting the ones to be read aloud. Their choices also tell you something about the themes that are really important to them and provide clues to situations on their minds. So pay attention to their preferences in stories as well as their comments and questions!

How can we include children of different ages?

Stories in this book have been rated by experts in children's literature as appropriate for children between the ages of four and nine. *Story Project* parents observed that younger children in this age group simply enjoyed listening to the stories. They were not too interested in discussing questions. Conversations about the stories developed an appeal with children from age six or seven to well beyond age nine. Older children often help younger children consider topics by offering their own experience as examples. Depending on the ages of your children, you may need to adjust the model to fit. If you have quite young children participating, keep the model simple. Read a story and say the prayer, shortening the reflection section to a statement or two. If you have younger *and* older children, let the little ones play after the story, perhaps in the same room, while the older children talk a little bit about their ideas. If your children are close in age – one or two years apart – make a little time available with each one to hear concerns out of earshot from brothers and sisters.

Children often enjoy using art as a way of responding to the story. A child can draw an idea in a picture even before that child could express that idea in words. Young children can illustrate their impressions of the story. Older children have produced interesting cartoons of stories for me, drawing four- or six-block comic strips that highlight different moments of the story. I find it interesting to hear children put the story in their own words. The ways in which children rephrase dialogue and express characters' feelings helps you hear the meaning of the story for them.

If you suggest drawing as an activity, take some time to have each child talk about his or her artwork. Talking about a picture you draw yourself can be easier than answering a direct question about the story. Because adults don't always see the meaning in a child's drawing clearly, start a conversation with an open-ended comment like "Tell me about your picture."

What if not all family members want to participate?

Family members often differ in experience and opinion from each other. This is true whether we speak about interest in sports, taste in television shows or belief in God. Parents with different religious views need to discuss how matters of faith and religious practice fit into the home they build together. Working with differences respectfully is an important example to set for children and reduces the opportunities to play one parent off against the other. Using this storytelling model does not depend on holding a particular view of Christian faith, nor does it advocate one Christian tradition. The stories have found appeal with a wide range of readers from many different churches, as well as with some who don't attend church at all. This feature may ease anxiety between adults whose views about faith differ.

The *Story Project* model invites all participants, adults and children alike, to speak from their own experience, sharing ideas and questions about what matters in life. Families who differ over the significance of faith may discover that this approach teaches children to consider and respect different opinions within the family and beyond. During the project, children who began to reflect on questions with one parent occasionally urged the other parent to join in. Children are curious about their parents' early experience. They also appreciate a chance to express their own opinions and be taken seriously.

If some family members remain reluctant to participate in storytelling and reflection, their hesitation should be respected. Force-feeding faith can call up the same resistance children muster to food they dislike. Lingering resistance in a child can be drawn out in a one-on-one conversation to discover what underlying concerns exist. Sometimes a child develops mistaken meaning about God on their own. Sometimes a child is nervous about speaking or acting in a new way. Gentle conversation can help a child name hidden concerns and reconsider them. Adults who feel hesitant to participate may want to explore the roots of their hesitation on their own. If you have a lingering question or sore point about God, it is important to pursue it. At the end of the book, I suggest a few resources to help adults address faith questions in personal study. Seeking out a knowledgeable minister, priest, church educator or spiritual director for private discussion can also help you address troubling questions or remembered experiences.

Dealing with feelings

Children often need help to express a feeling fully and accurately. When a child says she feels "bad," for example, what does "bad" mean? It could refer to feeling physically sick, feeling sad, being discouraged or having low self-esteem, among other things. Often such a feeling is rooted in a personal story that deserves to be heard by a receptive listener. We help children learn to interpret their feelings by offering them clear, accessible terms and phrases that express their current response to a story or situation. When talking about the feelings evoked by a story, you can offer choices for a child to consider if the child is struggling to express a response. Suggesting possibilities rather than giving a single opinion enables the child to think through options and pick the one that seems most fitting.

The index of feelings explored in various stories may be helpful when you want to explore how your children are feeling about a particular situation. When consulting that index, note the ways in which feelings are identified and interpreted. I have used terms that adults know rather than ones that children recognize. Categories like "low self-esteem," "uncertainty" or "relief" are identified. These are not terms for emotions but concepts that interpret the meaning of feelings in relation to a situation. When speaking with children about feelings, try to use simpler words or phrases to distinguish feelings.

When it comes to saying a prayer that expresses our feelings to God, invite your children to name their own feelings or interests in the words they choose for themselves. Each child and adult could offer a one-line prayer responding to the same story, holding up a combination of feelings and concerns. We all benefit from such a reminder that people feel differently about the same situation.

Can grandparents use these stories if a child's parents are not interested in faith or spiritual life?

In some families, grandparents have a keener interest in developing a grandchild's relationship with God than do the child's parents. This model of storytelling and reflection may offer a bridge between generations in such situations. Most stories in this collection do not focus on commitment to the Church but rather touch on ways in which we can know God and follow Jesus' example day by day. Children's questions about God are triggered as much by what they encounter every day as by specific teaching in church. Grandparents will find that these stories create small openings to talk about their faith with grand-children in practical ways. Parents who themselves prefer not to discuss faith will still find that these stories lift up important questions about values and human relations with which children struggle. Sharing the struggle is important, whether or not faith in God is mentioned.

Other suggestions for using this material at home

When your children are looking for rainy-day projects, encourage them to draw cartoons of a favourite story or to act out some of these adventures. When children claim their own storytelling ability and interpret one of these little dramas, you will see or hear the feelings and ideas in the story from a child's perspective. As a spectator to an improvised performance or imaginative drawing, you have a fresh opportunity to listen to your child's view of themselves and the world. Children can also be encouraged to write their own adventure stories, borrowing characters from this collection or inventing their own. Again, when you hear a child tell a new story, listen for any concerns or feelings woven into the story. Follow up with a question such as "Do you remember when something like that happened?"

Food for Thought –
Stirring Stories into Children's Programs

The resources collected in this book have not only been tested by parents at home, but also by teachers and leaders in congregational programs for children. Two congregations experimented by supplementing the educational material used each Sunday with stories from this collection. Another church used the stories in a children's liturgy that began the Sunday by Sunday program session. Other leaders tried out this model for opening or closing worship with mid-week children's groups. In workshops, I have also been asked about how to co-ordinate stories with catechism and with preparation for a child's first communion. *Story Project* resources are laid out in a straightforward, consistent model in this collection. Each story is followed by a reflection, a few questions to talk about and a short prayer. Here are some suggestions on how to use this material in different educational settings.

What could this storytelling model add to published curriculum materials for children?

The design of *The Story Project* material uses an educational approach called *praxis. Praxis* invites children to reflect on what happens to them in light of what we believe about God. Their reflections are expressed to God in prayer and to others in conversation. *Praxis* also leads participants to act in new or different ways because of what we believe and who we are as God's people. Both the reflection section and the questions that follow each story often include an opportunity for children to imagine what they can do for God and with God.

Published curriculum materials use a variety of educational approaches linked to the learning goals of each curriculum. Some emphasize learning Bible stories. Others concentrate on important elements in worship, church life and church teaching. Some combine these goals. All the goals are important if we want children to know their place as part of God's people. However, some curriculum designs do not draw on *praxis* models. Rather than inviting children to ask their own questions about God and to tell their own stories, a curriculum may concentrate on opportunities to learn the content of Scripture or church teaching. The model presented in this book can add elements to such resources, offering children opportunities to talk about what matters to them and perhaps to decide how to act on their faith and their concerns. It is a natural fit with curriculum material that uses a *praxis* approach, offering a wider range of possibilities to explore connections with curriculum themes.

The Story Project resources can supplement different kinds of curriculum in several ways. First, we'll look at ways to integrate these resources with Bible-focused materials. Then, I offer a few suggestions about working with programs that prepare children for participating in church life.

Working with a curriculum based on Bible stories and Scripture passages

There are many ways to teach the Bible to children. A curriculum may use one or more of the approaches described here. Sometimes a curriculum moves through "story cycles," the series of stories that teach us about a character or a time in the history of God's people. Figures like Moses, Joseph and David in the Old Testament and Jesus or Paul in the New Testament are known to us through story cycles that can be explored, story by story, over a number of weeks. Another curriculum approach also focuses on biblical characters but chooses stories according to a theme rather than a chronological cycle. For example, a unit of your curriculum might look at "The Women Who Knew Jesus," "People God Healed" or "People Who Took God's Dare." When working with either of these approaches, look at the characters in key episodes and consider the life situation presented. There may be an easy connection to draw, using the life situation index in Part Three. For example, the story *Fergie Gets a Surprise* introduces Fergie's baby sister and works through the feelings of jealousy that children sometimes feel when a new family member arrives. In the stories about Joseph, jealousy arises between Joseph and his older brothers – an important theme to explore in light of God's love for us and the purposes God accomplishes through us.

It is not always a direct move from a biblical situation into a contemporary child's world, however. Consider the connection between the story *Fergie Loses a Friend* and the Bible story in John 11, often called "The Raising of Lazarus." In John's Gospel, Jesus is called to heal his dying friend but arrives too late. Lazarus has died. His sisters are filled with sorrow and anger. So is Jesus. He stands at the tomb of his friend and weeps. Then he calls Lazarus to rise up. The life situation described in most detail in John's story is the deep sorrow caused by the death of a friend. I chose to write a story for children that evokes some of the sorrow and confusion we feel when someone in our life is gone. However, the life situation for Fergie is a little different. The story is not specifically about death – Fergie's friend is captured. Nor does the story move to the miracle recounted in the Gospel. Instead, the reflection and prayer seek to present Jesus' tears for Lazarus as God's tears for us when we are sad and scared. In Christian tradition this Gospel story moves from the face of Jesus to the face of God. John's story promises that God knows our sorrow and comes to be with us with things go wrong. The feelings identified in the biblical story are reflected in Fergie's story. When you are working with stories about biblical characters, pay attention to the feelings named in the Bible (if they are), but also to your own feelings and those children express. This is a key link between your curriculum and *Story Project* resources.

It is worth noting that most stories in this collection could be related to more than one specific Bible story. For example, *Fergie Loses a Friend* could be just as effective following the story when Joseph's brothers sell him to traders and then tell their father that Joseph was killed (Genesis 37). Their father was devastated by the loss of his son, not knowing it was a trick by the older brothers. Fergie's story touches such loss with our conviction that God draws near to us when things go wrong.

Another kind of curriculum design co-ordinates the biblical content for a children's program with weekly lectionary readings used in Sunday worship. A lectionary is an established set of Scripture readings given for each Sunday of the year as well as other important Christian festivals. Each week, lectionaries offer four Scripture readings: one each from the Old Testament, the Psalms, the New Testament letters and the Gospels. Many different churches of use the same lectionary these days. There are now many ecumenical lectionary curriculum resources that provide material to use with children as well as worship resources for the whole parish. The challenge for a children's program based on the lectionary is to draw from the four assigned readings something that a child can grasp. This is not always easy, especially if you are working with children of different ages in the same group.

If your curriculum is lectionary-based, look at the Scripture lesson to be highlighted each week. If a story from the Old or New Testament will be the focus for worship, then earlier comments about story cycles, feelings and life situations will help you find complementary stories. But if the theme for worship comes from a Scripture passage that does not tell a story, then the index of faith themes will be more helpful. Here's an example of how I developed a story related to a faith theme expressed in different parts of the Bible.

In the letters written by St. Paul, he often speaks about the diversity of people welcomed into the Body of Christ. We find this theme expressed in Romans 12, 1 Corinthians 12 and Galatians 3, for example. "Diversity" is a concept word young children won't understand. Yet they likely have some experience of feeling threatened or resentful when someone new arrives. They may have heard name-calling on the playground that emphasizes differences among children. The story from the Sherman the Hound Dog series called *Cat Attack!* draws these themes from the Bible and a child's life together. Lucy comes home with a cat she wants to keep for the weekend. Sherman is unhappy because, in his mind, cats and dogs don't get along. He doesn't want the cat around. The story playfully works out how Sherman comes to see the cat with new eyes. The faith themes listed recognize our relationship with "God our Maker": "God makes many different creatures" and "We are all special to God." Again, Sherman's story will fit with many other Bible stories. The theme that God loves those who are different from "us," whoever "we" are, is very important throughout the Bible. *Cat Attack!* helps children visualize and remember this important theme when the Scripture lesson doesn't provide a story that is easy to remember.

One of the challenges combining *Story Project* resources with published curriculum material is finding enough time in a session to fit things together. Congregations that tested this material in Sunday morning programs often found that reading both a Bible story *and* one of these animal stories took up too much time in a short session to do justice to either one. When I used *Story Project* material to supplement a lectionary-based curriculum, the minister told the Bible story for the week while the children were in the worship service. When the children and I left worship for our program, they discussed the Bible story with me for a few minutes. Then we used a story from this collection to relate a theme from the Bible story to our own lives. If you have just a short time available each week (45 minutes or less), then consider using this model once in a while as a way to connect the significance of Bible stories to our lives today. For example, if your class has looked at stories where biblical figures must find the courage to "take God's dare," the story *You Can Count on Fergie* could be used to sum up this theme by talking about the kind of courage a child needs when someone is being bullied.

Working with a curriculum on church teachings and children's participation in church life

Churches and publishers from specific Christian traditions develop other kinds of curriculum resources to prepare children to participate in the life of the Church. Such material helps children understand significant events that happen regularly in worship, such as baptism and Holy Communion. The commitments we make to follow Jesus are often taught in catechetical classes and in programs that explore moral values and social concerns. Children's activity groups may also explore the seasons of the church year, preparing crafts for Advent and Christmas or sharing in a mission project during Lent. The stories in this collection can also be co-ordinated with such published resources using the indexes in Part III. Here are a few suggestions to help you relate these stories to themes in other material.

Preparing children for baptism or first communion

To be baptized or to receive communion for the first time is a tremendously significant moment in a child's spiritual life. Different churches offer these opportunities to children at different ages and in different ways. For example, in churches that welcome infants for baptism, children may well see the baptism of a brother or sister rather than prepare for their own. Some children prepare to receive communion with a group of their peers, others at a time when they feel ready. The material in this collection is appropriate to help children up to age nine talk about the themes in Christian life commonly associated with baptism and communion. It can be used in groups or one-on-one. The stories do not take a doctrinal position on baptism or communion. However, they can be co-ordinated by faith theme with the teachings presented in approved church resources.

In the faith theme index in Part III, you will find statements that connect stories to topics usually associated with baptism or communion. For example, when we think about baptism, several themes in the index come to mind: "God loves us," "God forgives us," "We belong to God," "We are special to God." Preparation for communion would include themes about Jesus' self-giving (for example, "Jesus shows us God's love") and about the church ("We are part of God's family"). Both baptism and communion connect our lives in Church to life in the world, so look for stories on the themes "We care for God's world" and "We help each other" to link the sacraments with Christian service. When you are presenting such important themes to children, remember that children work with familiar experience to make connections with new ideas. Stories help children build these connections. Reflections and prayers draw children from familiar experience towards the more mysterious ways in which we meet God. Use the children's insights recorded in Chapter 2 to anticipate questions that concern children about God's presence with us and the gifts that Jesus offers.

Be sure in your times of preparation that children have opportunity to ask their own questions. They will have questions about the teaching of Church but also about "what happens when" during baptism or communion. Sometimes a child will feel anxious before taking such an important step in public worship. If you sense that a child preparing for baptism or first communion is nervous, look up stories in the index of feelings under "worry," "fear" or "uncertainty." The prayers that accompany these stories may help children learn to cope with anxiety as time draws near. Often such anxiety is fed by uncertainty about what the child's role will be. Spend enough time talking and walking through what each child is expected to do!

Combining stories with catechism resources

Several Christian traditions use catechisms to introduce children to important teachings of their Church. Combining stories with a catechism uses the same strategy described above for preparing children for baptism or communion. Work by faith theme to find a story that dramatizes a catechism theme from a child's perspective. The index of life situations may also be useful to talk about how we act as Jesus' disciples. This index highlights situations most children encounter and sometimes find challenging. Being a disciple of Jesus takes commitment. It is as challenging today as it was long ago. Stories can prepare children to make choices based on their faith in God when faced with new situations.

Using stories to talk about Christian values and Christian service

The stories in this collection often raise dilemmas of childhood for discussion. In this way, they connect well with resources designed to teach children about moral values and making choices. These stories can be used to explore a range of themes related to personal issues as well as larger social issues. The life situation index will be most helpful if you want to talk about particular values or situations where a child faces a moral dilemma. When talking about values with young children, it is important to work with concrete situations rather than abstract terms for values. It is also important to talk about the feelings we have when we face a moral choice. *Finders Keepers?* tells of the choice Jackie Rabbit faces when she finds a purse that someone has lost. Losing and finding are familiar territory for many children, and the story opens up the theme of *temptation* in a way children can discuss. It also opens up another difficult challenge. Jackie Rabbit is hungry. Her temptation is related to her need. Helping children recognize the needs of people in their communities is also important. This story might also lead to a conversation about how people care for each other when some are hungry and some have food to share.

The concerns expressed by children in Chapters 2 and 3 demonstrate that they are ready to talk about what they can do to live out God's love in the world. Use the questions after a story to open up conversations on this theme. *Fergie Cleans Up* raises questions related to caring for the earth, for example. Service projects in the church or community give children an opportunity to live out their faith, to make a visible contribution to their neighbourhoods, and also to observe in concrete ways the impact of thoughtless behaviour. Moving from conversation to action is an important commitment for the followers of Jesus, no matter what our age!

What other kinds of activities can be used with these stories?

Art provides a good follow-up to a story, even before you talk about it. It gives younger children something active to do before you ask them to focus on questions. It also provides the leader with an opportunity to talk one-on-one with children about what they are drawing. Children can illustrate the stories in comic strip fashion, or make collages to express how a story makes them feel. If you are dealing with a mixed age group, you may want to offer a range of craft activities to follow up a story. Small children might draw or make modelling clay figures. Older children can write their own stories or develop their own endings to these stories to illustrate what they would do if they were the main character. Children also enjoy acting out stories and developing the plots a little further.

When I have done such storytelling art and activities with children, I have been impressed by two things. First, children have an amazing ability to shape stories and illustrate the plots of situations that they themselves have experienced. Even quite young children can fill in the frames of a comic strip to tell a story they've just heard or to narrate in pictures something that happened to them. The ways their own plots resolve is an interesting indicator of how children interpret their faith in God. Secondly, children who are a bit reluctant to speak out in a group often share a small but important insight when they can deliver their ideas directly to the teacher's ear. I always take time to hear each class member describe their picture or talk about their story one-on-one.

How do children of different ages in the same group respond to these stories?

Mixed-age groups represent special challenges because children's ways of thinking and using language change so much between the ages of four and nine. Yet parishes with small numbers of children often face the need to teach them as a single group. Where the age span is more than a year or two in your class or group, take care not to let the learning of the older children overwhelm the younger ones. When inviting responses from a diverse group, mix up the ages of the respondents as you invite children to speak. Let some of the younger ones speak first if they are ready. Identify and affirm common themes that emerge in children's comments as well as the special examples that children with unique experience raise. Remember that children learn a lot from each other in mixed-age groups. Try to affirm the feeling or the insight in each response and recognize the genuine interest in every question, even the ones that may seem a bit odd!

How can a leader respond to difficult questions or comments raised by a story?

These stories explore the presence of God in our lives and ways in which we can seek God's help. They avoid explanations. If a child's question seeks an explanation about God or God's way of working, ask the child first to say a little more about his or her own thinking on the question. You may find a truth or a feeling or an experience you can affirm. Or you may then see how to set what you believe alongside the child's current thinking. Children will continue to puzzle about matters of faith, so don't be afraid that you have to offer the "right" answer right away. Respecting and receiving children's questions is one of the most important ways to encourage their faith to develop.

If your class or group meets regularly, turn a good question into an opportunity for everyone to learn how to explore a question. See the suggestions for responding to children's questions near the end of Chapter 2. Think about how to use the church library or the Internet for research, and challenge children to report on what they discover. Invite resource people in your congregation and community to puzzle through a question with many angles. Questions about faith open a door for much learning and growth for children and leader alike.

Some of these stories raise serious topics for reflection. When inviting children to respond with stories of their own, also take care to offer children the right to decline comment. If an experience is too raw or if a child fears the judgment of others, that child ought not to be put on the spot. Listen to questions a child raises in light of what you know about that child's situation. For example, could a question about heaven be connected to a death in the family that the child is worried about? This might be a cue that a one-on-one pastoral conversation is needed. As a leader, you might be able to arrange for someone with appropriate skills to follow up. Once in a while a child makes a puzzling reference that may concern a teacher about the child's welfare or family situation. Make sure that leaders in your program know how to follow up such a concern appropriately with church or community authorities. Having a strategy to respond to children's health and safety needs is an important responsibility for all church leaders.

Bread for the Journey – Sampling Stories in Worship Settings

Storytelling, reflection and prayer have long been central aspects of Christian worship through which God's Spirit engages us in many ways. Participating in worship also involves some habits of heart, mind and body that prepare us to respond in prayer and wonder. Children learn the habits or patterns of participation informally as they join with the whole community in Sunday services. They move and are still, they sing and pray, they speak and listen in rhythm with the gathered congregation. A child's ability to share in this rhythm grows as the child does. The stories, reflections and prayers in this collection aim to encourage children to develop certain worshipful practices – listening, reflecting and praying – by connecting those abilities to themes that are meaningful to children.

Because the stories set up situations to which children readily respond, children begin to listen attentively. Simple statements and questions invite children to reflect on common situations and consider their own choices and challenges. The prayers use words that children themselves use, inviting them to pray in everyday language. These worshipful practices are not the only things children need to share deeply in the life of the Church. However, they are aspects of worship that believers of every age can cultivate. They are not childish things to be outgrown; they are abilities that grow with the child, enriching faith through encounters with God.

This model of storytelling and reflecting with children can be integrated into various patterns of liturgy to enrich children's experience of Sunday worship. Each local church is a little different from every other church, even within the same tradition. Space, time and leadership are obvious and important aspects of your church worship that no resource manual can address precisely. Following are some questions and concerns raised by storytellers and worship leaders who have used these resources in worship, as well as a few of my own observations after telling stories in many different churches. Let these comments inspire you to look at your own situation with new eyes.

How can these stories fit into a weekly Sunday service?

This model of storytelling was developed for Sunday worship that included a brief time for a children's story early in the service. Children gathered with me at the front of the sanctuary for a story and prayer. There are many other ways for children to participate in worship, of course. Let me suggest a few ways in which these resources can fit into a Sunday service.

1. *Include a brief time for storytelling with children within congregational worship.* If the order of service provides a brief time specifically to speak with children about their concerns, these resources can easily be adapted. Because these stories develop themes from both faith and life, they can be selected to fit with other aspects of the service or the season of the Christian year. Each story with its brief reflection and prayer can be read expressively in about eight minutes. If you choose to ask children a question or two, time can expand quickly! Estimating the time needed for children to participate effectively is important in worship planning. The younger the listeners, the briefer and more focused such a time should be. Stories can be edited, dropping a few words here and there, when time is of the essence. For a brief time of storytelling, I gather children together in an appropriate place. In some churches using this model, children who have gathered for a story then leave the sanctuary together for a program. If children stay in the sanctuary for the whole service, gathering them for a story allows them to

expend some restless energy coming and going. Work with your church musician to choose music to help children move in appropriate ways.

2. *Use stories for "all-age" worship occasions.* Some of the longer stories in this collection have been used for all-age worship services on specific themes. Here are some suggestions on how to work with a longer story so that young children continue to engage it and adults can deepen their reflection on the theme.

- *Spread stories out.* Two stories, *Fergie Gets a Surprise* and *The Advent Adventure of Jackie Rabbit*, are divided into three shorter episodes that I spaced throughout a service. Children gathered with me for each story and prayer, and then returned to their families while we sang and listened to Scripture. Hymns, scripture readings and prayers were chosen to deepen the reflection and response for adult listeners.

- *Highlight the theme of the story throughout the service.* For example, *Fetch!* is a story on different ways of praising. In a worship service on this theme, the worship leaders can introduce different steps in the liturgy to highlight how or why we praise God through our next act of worship.

- *Link the story to issues of concern in your parish community.* The story *How Big Is This Family?* explores the challenge of making room for newcomers in the family and in the Church. This story might be combined with short presentations by newcomers to the parish who relate a moment when someone helped them feel welcome.

In all-age worship, it is important to offer some aspect of the service that touches the interest of each generation present, relating these aspects through the theme for the day. A colleague used these materials for Sunday worship in which children participated throughout the liturgy with the adults. He chose a story on the faith theme for the service that guided his choice of readings, prayers and songs. Following a story, he began a conversation with the children and then briefly summarized the theme in a few thought-provoking sentences for adult listeners. This informal, interactive style of leadership worked well in the small church he serves. He has found that people of all ages respond to the links between the Bible readings and contemporary life opened up by these stories.

Another worship team developed "readers' theatre" presentations from these stories, using different people for each character and for the narrator. This approach appealed to many in the congregation when it was used on a couple of special all-age occasions. Preparations involved a lot of people from the whole congregation, as well as a few homemade costumes and props to help the youngest listeners pay attention. Organizers agreed, however, that this kind of presentation would not have sustained its appeal in that congregation every Sunday.

3. *Use stories in children's liturgies.* When children gather together for worship, these stories can provide a homily or reflection when chosen to fit the faith theme for the day. Use the faith theme index or the life situation index to find stories for a specific occasion or Bible reading. If a group is relatively small in proportion to the number of leaders present, you might like to use a question or two in response to the story for a short discussion. But if a group is large or the mix of ages quite broad, discussing questions won't be very fruitful or worshipful. When children worship together, expand the prayer time that follows a story. Invite children to name concerns for prayer inspired by the story. Or give them a moment to compose a prayer sentence or two that they can offer aloud when the prayer begins.

How do I choose a story from Part II of this book?

Part II contains more than twenty stories. To choose an appropriate one, look in the margins for explanatory notes, which describe the faith theme, life situation, feelings and, in some cases, connection to the Church year for each story. Feel free to write your own notes in the margins as well to help you remember when you used a particular story and how it worked. It may be helpful to note how children responded to the phrasing of questions, if you use any, and to note any interesting comments you hear in response to the story. Comments help to identify the themes and the feelings children identify for themselves. In this way you can build on your experience as you work your way through the stories.

The indexes in Part III will also help you choose a story to suit a theme or situation you want to explore with children. The stories are indexed according to life situations, feelings and biblical references. Spending some time with the indexes will allow you to see many possibilities!

How can these stories be co-ordinated with lectionary readings?

I began to write these stories when I was preaching each week from Scripture lessons suggested in the *Common Lectionary*, an ecumenical resource then in wide use. After I prepared my sermon based on one of the Bible lessons for the week, I considered a child's view of the theme that had emerged from my interpretation of Scripture. I resist the temptation to provide a lectionary index for these stories, however. I value the leading of the Holy Spirit when I interpret Scripture, whether I am looking at a passage for the first time or the fifteenth time. I could not presume to name which theme or question will emerge from fresh interpretation of a biblical text in a unique pastoral setting.

Each story has both a faith theme and a life situation that may connect with a concern identified in biblical readings, whether chosen from the lectionary or another way. There is also an index identifying the feelings evoked by a story. When I'm preparing a service or a sermon, I sometimes consider what feelings surround a biblical story or theme. I choose a story for children that creates that feeling. Then my reflection and prayer consider how our faith in God helps us work with that feeling in the middle of situations like the one presented in the story. Look at the examples given above in the *Food for Thought* section in "*Working with a curriculum based on Bible stories and Scripture passages*" to see other ways to move between the interpretation of Scripture and storytelling.

As I preached through the cycles of the lectionary in different congregations, I often found that a story I had written for a previous occasion also fit with themes raised by other biblical texts. Stories have many layers. The feeling or the situation considered in a story can be viewed from many angles. A different reflection or prayer might be required, so feel free to develop your own follow-up to a story, informed by different theological or biblical insights. Just remember to keep your words simple and concrete when you offer a reflection, ask a question or lead a prayer. Stick to a single theme. An adult can see the complexity in a simple statement. Children cannot accurately simplify an idea that is too complex for their current understanding.

A few stories in this collection were prepared for specific seasons or Sundays in the church year. In Advent, for example, I wrote a continuing adventure series that ended as a "cliff-hanger" each week. Its purpose was to feel our way through the Advent theme of waiting. (See *The Advent Adventures of Jackie Rabbit.*) This approach often brought children back to church, week by week, parents in tow, in order to find out what happened next! I lifted the mounting suspense in prayer with children, seeking God's help whenever we find ourselves frustrated or uncertain. Children know by experience that life's complexities do not resolve overnight, so they need to trust the companionship of God in the midst of situations that are not yet resolved.

Is it important to use one of these stories in worship every week?

Yes and no. Young children respond to ritual as a way of ordering their world. A familiar pattern helps them understand how they are expected to respond. Children come to rely on their experience week by week in worship. They grow in connection with characters they meet regularly in stories. Such children are sensitive to change within the liturgy because they cannot readily anticipate new expectations. However, balanced with the importance of ritual familiar to children is the wonder of God's surprising movement among and within us. All worshippers can learn to adapt to new ways of participating in worship from time to time, sensing something fresh as a gift of the Spirit.

When worship planners consider the sweep of worship throughout a season or a year, different models of participation by children can be developed. If certain months or seasons are set aside for storytelling, at other times make room for other kinds of presentations by and for children. As you lay out long-term plans, keep an eye on how children in your congregation are supported and encouraged to develop the fullest worship life possible. If children only experience one short part of a worship service regularly, they will not know how to participate in the full service. However, changing the models of children's participation in worship too often can be confusing for young children and those new to your congregation. Whenever you introduce changes, whether by adding or eliminating a story or by offering a different kind of worship experience, prepare the children with a straightforward introduction. Help them anticipate what is expected of them so they can participate as fully as possible without feeling self-conscious. Don't over-explain the change, however, or children get confused.

Another consideration in choosing when or how often to tell a story arises from a basic understanding of why we worship. Every worship service invites us to draw closer to God and to express our praise to God. Though I love to tell stories, it is my personal discipline not to insist on storytelling every week. Otherwise, storytelling could become a way of drawing attention to me. The entertainment value of a story can subtly assert itself if storytelling is not linked theologically and pastorally to a congregation's worship life.

Who should tell these stories in worship?

The role of storyteller in the life of young children is quite special in ways not immediately obvious to adults. There is a kind of aura around storytellers from a child's perspective. I encounter this whenever I give public readings of my stories or greet children after a worship service in which I have told a story. In a congregation where I had served but moved on, a four-year-old girl asked her mother, "When will we have a real minister again?" Her mother assured her that the man leading worship was a minister. "No," said the little girl, "a real minister is a lady with puppets." The role of storyteller is not to be taken lightly! Those who plan worship should think carefully about who in the pastoral and educational lives of children appropriately bears the storytelling role.

As a pastor, I cherished the brief opportunity each week to speak and pray with the children of the congregation. It gradually dawned on me that these short times were clearing pastoral pathways to my door that children followed, often unbeknownst to their parents. Ministers who tell stories to children regularly in worship are establishing pastoral relationships with those children that have significance outside worship. Still, I know some ministers who are uncomfortable working with children. Storytelling with children is not their gift. If stories are used in worship where a pastor is not a storyteller, that pastor can sit with the children as a participant observer, sharing the storytime as a listener, perhaps leading them in prayer. A pastoral gate is opened when someone is seen to be a good listener!

Storytelling in worship is a role for those who have both gifts and passion for this old art form. Perhaps each year a small core of storytellers could be chosen from the congregation, people with whom the children will become familiar. The minister may or may not be part of this core. Familiarity creates better listening on both sides. This core of storytellers can work on skills for good storytelling appropriate to the particular worship space in which they function. Speaking effectively for the space and for the occasion is an important skill to cultivate by offering supportive feedback to each other.

Is it a good idea to discuss a story with children during worship?

Pursuing answers to questions with children during worship, whatever resources are used, has many risks. Sometimes a child blurts out something inappropriate and then feels bad. Parents may also be embarrassed. Picking one or two children to answer can leave others disappointed. A clown will occasionally make a silly remark, enjoying adult reactions. None of these responses is particularly worshipful. Children also deserve the same pastoral consideration and discretion adults expect. The reflection sections sometimes include a rhetorical question to think about. An unanswered question keeps ideas percolating. I use questions in a sermon with adult listeners in a similar way. With both children and adults, I have found that conversations emerge after someone has time to mull over an important question.

How do adults respond to these stories in worship?

Sometimes adults comment that they "get more out of the children's story than the sermon." This is a reminder to preachers and worship leaders that we are all influenced by the communication styles popular in today's culture. Storytelling carries the power to create visual images for the listener in ways that make its message both easy to grasp and memorable. Stories connect with adults in ways that are more accessible than other forms of teaching and preaching. The stories in this collection often ring true with adults as they remember their growing-up years. I found that by linking my stories thematically with my sermons, my preaching became more accessible for many listeners. These stories can provide a concrete step into more serious theological reflection among adult worshippers.

To laugh or not to laugh?

Is humour welcome in your worship setting? This is a consideration when choosing material from this collection. There are details and twists in these little tales that make both children and adults laugh. Some people enjoy a lighthearted story in worship, while others may consider the same story inappropriate or disrespectful. As a theologian, I think humour has an appropriate place in our life of faith. A comic insight or a humorous exchange often probes human limitations and life's complexities. Humour can also rearrange our expectations, just as Jesus' parables do. When humour is wise or delightful, it speaks of the wisdom and goodness of God. When humour is playful, it must respect its audience and not play people against each other or downplay their significance to God. I hope readers will find the humour in these stories true to these convictions. If adult listeners are troubled by humour, then the opportunity to reflect theologically on God's gift of laughter is in order! However, let your choice of stories take into account the place of humour in the worshipping style of your congregation.

To see or not to see?

Another practical dimension that can shape adult reactions is whether everyone can hear and see what is happening. If children gather to hear a story some distance from the rest of the congregation, make sure that the storyteller's voice carries well. If a story is truly part of worship for the whole community, then it should be audible to the whole community. But being able to see and hear is only one test of "fit" for telling a story in a worship space. As a guest preacher, I once told a story using a puppet in a huge sanctuary designed on a formal cathedral pattern. About ten children gathered with me at the chancel steps. I was suddenly overwhelmed by the physical gulf between us and the other worshippers. I also realized that this conversational model worked at odds with the formality of the architecture and the liturgy. If I had been serving that congregation regularly, I would have had to reconsider the effectiveness of telling these stories in that physical space and formal liturgy.

Ingredients for Effective Storytelling

Gathering your listeners

Storytelling with children can be done in the intimate bond of a small circle or in the dramatic space of chancel or stage. When telling stories in the worship space, help children learn where and how to take their places. In some churches where I have told stories, the children simply charge forward, some running or pushing, others getting dragged along. If this scene is familiar in your church, consider taking time in worship to work with children on moving in holy space. This can be done over a few weeks, using the action of gathering as the focus for a conversation. How do we walk and worship at the same time? Attention to this theme could help children and adults experience reverence in new ways and teach worshipful actions that can grow with children. The book *Young Children and Worship* by Sonja Stewart and Jerome Berryman describes a very effective approach to help young children respect holy space.[13] Though presented within their unique design for worship and storytelling, the ways they describe to inspire reverence and respect for space could be adapted to teach children how to move in the sanctuary with regard for holy time and space.

When you gather children to listen to a story, seat them facing the storyteller. Then facial expressions and eye contact will hold a child's attention more effectively. If children sit beside a storyteller, strung along chancel steps facing the congregation, for example, those who are furthest away are most easily distracted. If you add a visual component to the story – a puppet or a drawing or some pictures – be sure to practise your presentation so that all listeners can see comfortably. Otherwise some children will struggle to see and break the concentration of those around them.

Strategies for telling a story to a group

A good storyteller always knows the story inside out and is involved with its plot so that the words come alive for the listeners. Practising the story out loud, pacing it well, and adding emphasis in voice, gesture and facial expression make a story more engaging. I often distinguish characters by using different voices, a technique children appreciate. The style of the storyteller has to respond to the size of the space and the proximity of young listeners, however. If children are sitting very close to the storyteller, be careful not to overwhelm small children with sounds that are too loud or energy that is too vigorous. I am more animated when standing a metre or two away from a group of listeners than when I'm seated with my listeners close to me. When the storyteller is seated, the story takes a little longer to tell because of the need to project carefully for those listeners sitting farther away in the worship space. When using a microphone to tell a story, be sure that it picks up your voice as you move your head around to look at all your listeners.

Should a storyteller memorize a story? Knowing a story by heart frees you to use gesture and movement in ways that can make a story come alive. However, I don't always have time to prepare to tell an unfamiliar story this way. I read it aloud several times beforehand so that I am not tied to the text, but I keep the text with me. Many children are used to hearing stories read from a book. They respond to the story whether it is read or told. If you are reading from a text, be sure to hold the text at an angle so that your voice carries over it and doesn't drop into your lap. This also allows you to look at your listeners as you read and keep face-to-face connection.

Working with young listeners of different ages

If very young children (ages 2 and 3) are included in a group gathering to sit with the storyteller, it is wise to have some older children or adults alerted to help the youngest ones come along and find a good place to sit. Newcomers also need some subtle direction or encouragement their first few times in worship. Prepare a few leaders among your listeners to help others get seated and to keep focused on the story. I depend on such assistants, whether children or adults, to maintain quiet and stillness for listening. I have found that once a group of children develops the general desire to listen to a story especially for them, the children themselves will quiet distracting neighbours.

Consider the age range of your listeners and the ratio of younger to older children. If your listeners include even a few children age four and younger, a visual prop like a puppet or a picture helps keep those with short attention spans focused. If your listeners are mostly very young, once the story ends move as quickly as possible to the prayer. Summarize the reflection in one or two sentences. If more children are of school age, you can be more flexible after the story with questions or the reflection. When you practise the story out loud, time yourself. A story that runs much over five minutes will need editing if you are working with listeners under age four.

To focus the attention of a mixed-age group, briefly introduce the theme of the story before you tell it. A comment or a question can focus novice listeners' attention in a gentle way. If some aspect of the story could be a little scary or sad for your listeners, prepare them for how they might feel. Remember the story *Fearless Fergie* from Chapter 1? Whenever I tell it, I begin by asking "Is anyone here afraid of the dark?" Usually, only the very youngest child admits such a fear with a little nod. Whatever response I get to my question, I always admit that I am sometimes afraid. (This is true!) In the middle of that story, however, just about everybody in the room is holding their breath. The prayer releases that tension to God. Setting up a difficult theme in advance allows children to cope with their reactions to the story as it unfolds.

Using puppets, pictures and props

Early in my ministry of storytelling, I acquired puppets for the characters whose stories form this collection. Children under four listened so much better with a puppet in view. Using puppets requires greater familiarity with the story. You can't turn pages easily with a puppet on one hand! The puppets I use are quite simple. Most have moving mouths or heads that tilt to add expression to the story. For a puppet that doesn't move very much, I sometimes add a piece of clothing or a prop related to the story. Puppets work well when the storyteller is fairly close to all listeners. If you gather children to listen to a puppet story, remember that some listeners will compete to sit as close as possible to the puppet.

During *The Story Project*, we used stories without illustrations. Parents of young children commented that pictures usually help their children follow the story. By age five or six, most children are capable of imagining the action for themselves. I believe we need to encourage children to use their imaginations so that they are not captive to the visual images that saturate the media. An animated storyteller doesn't need pictures, puppets or props to work with children effectively. If you would like to use illustrations while telling these stories, here are a few points to keep in mind:

1. Pictures add extra time to storytelling. Every listener wants a glimpse of each picture, a long enough glimpse to take in the message of the picture. You will need to sit or stand in a place that allows you to present illustrations in a slow sweep of the whole group.
2. If you want to create illustrations for these stories, invite artistic people in your church to create one or two large pictures per story,

featuring a key scene. One artist could create a common image of a character. Many artists could offer different interpretations of the same character. Or invite the children themselves to illustrate the stories. They will listen attentively to see when and how their illustrations are used.

3. Develop one large picture that portrays the key scene for the whole story. At the appropriate moment, have someone set it on an easel where every listener can see it. The storyteller can slow down briefly to allow children to study the picture but is freed of the need to handle many illustrations.

Using puppets, pictures or props makes rehearsal important. The storyteller must use such features comfortably or else they become distractions. You may want to get some feedback from a few volunteers who watch you practise in the space for storytelling. Can your visuals be seen everywhere the children are seated? How effective are they for the rest of the congregation? Does your voice carry well? (Sometimes a storyteller talks *to* a puppet, directing the voice away from listeners.) Where will you set the puppet or prop when the story is finished?

Praying with a group of children

When I pray with a group of children after a story, I speak a bit more slowly. I want to give children time to remember their own connections with the story. Sometimes children repeat a prayer phrase by phrase after the storyteller. This practice gives children an experience of prayer on their own lips, in words they know and can use themselves in other situations. However, a colleague pointed out a hidden shortcoming in this way of praying. Having used this model of prayer in her worship time with children for quite a while, she began to hear children repeating phrases after her in every other prayer during the service. The children were simply praying as they had been taught. A "children's prayer" ought not to set children apart from adults during worship. If one special prayer after a story is to be repeated line by line, adults should join children in praying this way. That way the whole congregation continues to pray together while children learn to distinguish the many ways we pray in worship.

With the prayers provided after each story in this collection, you will need to make a choice about pronouns depending on your setting. Some of the stories use prayers voiced in the first person: "Dear God, I'm glad to be your friend." "When I'm sad, come and be with me." Other prayers use "we" and "us" to place both praise and problems before God: "Help us to look after your world." If you are using these stories and their prayers with a child one-on-one or in a very small group, using the first person format will be appropriate. With bigger groups of children in more public settings, or perhaps when a whole family has gathered, choosing to use "we" and "us" gathers all people present together in the concern you offer God. Plural pronouns show children that they are not alone in their feelings or in trying to sort out life as faithful people. When I developed these prayers for public worship settings, I always used "we" and "us." Feel free to edit the pronouns in the prayers following each story to suit your setting and the situation of participating children. You may also be led by the Spirit to make up a prayerful response to the story yourself!

A Place at the Table

When I was growing up, I had my own place at the kitchen table. I sat there for every meal. Even as an adult returning to my parents' home, I usually took up that familiar place. But I had a place at our table in a different sense as well. My parents included us children in mealtime conversation. Whether the topic was local politics, daily events or family plans, my sister and I listened and chimed in from time to time. I learned a great deal about life and decision making at the supper table. My parents' practice stood in contrast to the old saying: "Children should be seen and not heard," which was a common view in earlier generations of Canadian culture. Some cultures still hold it as a norm for children's behaviour; I am glad that it was not the norm for my family. My parents had regard for what we said. We learned to think out our views and discuss them when we were still quite young because we had a place at the family table.

Regarding Children is a wonderful book about Christian family life written by pastoral theologian Herbert Anderson with Susan Johnson.[14] He invites families and church communities to think about the kind of regard they show for the children in their midst. In a home where a child knows he or she is welcome, the child learns healthy self-regard. Children can greet others with confidence when they know their place is secure. At home, the family of faith sets the table around which we discover in a deep and lasting way who we are and who welcomes us. We bring our questions and our crises home to face them with our families. Anderson builds from his interest in the family at home to the wider family of faith in local churches. Churches are also challenged to welcome children and give regard to their concerns and ideas. How children are invited to share in worship, how their interests are voiced in prayer and in parish commitments communicates the kind of regard leaders have for young lives. This regard, this welcome, will also speak of how we believe God regards children. We must ask ourselves whether the children around us know through our actions and commitments that God has set a place at the table for them.

Anderson finds his model for regarding children in Jesus. Jesus singled out a child as a symbol of God's kingdom at a time when children were regarded as little more than slaves or possessions. Jesus bestowed both place and value on children. His action emphasized that each person is unique and precious to God, no matter how young or how old. In the stories of Jesus, God's "kingdom" is pictured breaking into our world at mealtime. Jesus sat down to eat with tax collectors and sinners. He ate with friends and with people who resented him. A little boy's lunch was blessed to feed a hungry crowd. Bread and wine were blessed at table with Jesus' friends to feed the faith of all generations. People will come from east and west, from north and south to sit at table in God's kingdom, Jesus said. Children have a place in that kingdom, too. They deserve a place at our tables, the tables where we eat and where we meet.

The Story Project invites children to take their places at the table in God's family. This model of storytelling, conversation and prayer encourages children to regard themselves as people whose place in the world matters to God and to God's people. Its goal is to hear each other speak of what matters deeply to us and to the God who loves us. The conversations we encourage about what really matters to children become opportunities for God to speak to them – and through them. I hope you have heard God moving in the lives of the children we've listened to in these pages. I hope the conversations we've sampled have stimulated your own reflections on who God is for you and for all of us with a story to tell. When home and church receive each child as someone whom God invites to the banquet of faith, God honours our faithfulness. When we feast on story and prayer together, we will know God as our strength in our struggles and as our song of joy, whatever our age.

The table is set. Your place is ready. Stories await – in this book, in your life, and in each child's life that touches yours. Taste and see what good things God provides through the stories we tell one another.

Part II

The Story Collection

Presenting Fergie the Frog

You Can Count on Fergie

Fergie the Frog hopped home from school one day. "Hey, Mom!" he called. "There's a new kid in my class at school. Do you think I could bring her home for supper sometime?"

"Who's your new girlfriend, Fergie?" his mother teased as she stirred the spider legs into the stew.

"Mo-o-om, Tanya Turtle is *not* my girlfriend," Fergie declared. "But she is the greatest in math! She said she would help me with my times tables. So I thought maybe you could make flyloaf and mashed mushrooms with gravy one day soon. Flyloaf is Tanya's favourite!"

"I see," said Mother Frog. "I guess when you're seven, math is more important than romance. Flyloaf it is! How about Friday?"

"Mo-o-om! I am *not* in love with Tanya Turtle. I just like her. Okay?" Fergie grinned.

On Friday after school, Tanya and Fergie set off for the swamp.

"Thanks for inviting me for supper," said Tanya. "It's hard making friends at this school. Lots of frogs tease me because I'm a turtle and I can't hop very well. Actually, I can't hop at all!"

"That's okay, Tanya. You can do math all right. And that's what counts," said Fergie. "Heh, heh, heh!"

Tanya giggled. "Good one, Fergie!"

All of a sudden, three big frogs jumped out of the bushes and blocked their path. "Hey, Fergie, you got a new girlfriend?" one of them said in a mean voice.

Faith theme:
We are Jesus' friends.
We can help each other.

Life situation:
Facing a bully

Feelings:
Fear, courage

147

"Guess she couldn't move fast enough to get away from you," another croaked.

"C'mon, you guys," said Fergie. "Leave us alone."

"Or did you sweep her off her feet?" the third frog teased. He hopped right over Tanya. "Nah, couldn't be. It would take more than a pint-sized tadpole like Fergie to get this tub of a turtle off her feet. Let's give her a hand!"

The three big bully frogs flipped Tanya the Turtle onto her back. Tanya pulled her legs and her head inside her shell and lay in the middle of the path.

"Help me, Fergie. I can't turn myself over," Tanya cried from inside her shell.

Fergie hopped to Tanya's side. "Hey, leave her alone," he said to the bullies. "She wasn't hurting you."

"Maybe we should stick you in there with her," said one of the big frogs. He grabbed a stick and hopped towards Fergie. "Come here, you little tad-poke!"

Fergie took off, hopping as fast as he could.

One of the bullies shouted, "Look at that little green flea hop! What about your girlfriend, Fergie?"

When Fergie got home, Mother Frog was just putting the flyloaf in the oven. "Where's your friend?" she asked.

"Quick, Mom! Quick, Freddie! We have to go save Tanya from a gang of big bully frogs. Follow me!" Fergie called.

When the three of them reached Tanya the Turtle, the bullies were gone.

"Tanya, it's okay. It's me, Fergie, with my mom and my brother, Freddie. We'll flip you right side up!" Then the three frogs gently flipped Tanya over.

When she was back on her feet again, Tanya said, "Thanks for coming back, Fergie. When I heard you hopping away, I thought you were gone for good. You saved me from turning into turtle soup!"

Fergie blushed a little. "Well, Tanya," he said, "I may not be very good at math, but you can always count on me!"

"Good one, Fergie," Tanya giggled.

Reflecting on the story

Friends are people we can count on – to help us with little problems like math, or to be there when we're in big trouble. Jesus calls us his friends. We can count on him to be with us when we're in trouble, and his love can help us to be good friends for other people to count on.

Talking about the story

- Has something like this ever happened to you or one of your friends? How did things turn out?
- Who are the friends you can count on?
- What could you do to help if you saw some-one being teased, bullied or pushed around?

Praying after the story

Jesus, I am glad to be your friend. Be there with me when I have problems big or small. Help me remember that I can count on your love to make things better. Amen.

Fergie's Best Friend

Faith theme:
With God's love,
we can be good
friends.

Life situation:
When our friend
finds a new friend

Feelings:
Jealousy

One day, Fergie the Frog hopped home from school very excited.

"What's new?" asked Mother Frog as she peeled the cattails for stew.

"I made a new friend today. He's fantastic! He's the biggest frog in our class. He tells great jokes. He's the best swimmer. And he gave me one of his toad jam tarts at lunch."

"Sounds like quite a frog!" said Fergie's mother. "What's his name?"

"Bill Frog. But I get to call him Bull. That's his nickname," Fergie explained.

Fergie did everything with his new friend, Bull. They sailed lily pads in the swamp. They explored the creek. They ate mosquito ripple ice cream.

A few days later, Fergie's mother said, "Roger called to see you this afternoon."

"Roger? Oh, Roger. What did he want? He knew Bull and I were practising our dives at the old rock." Fergie frowned.

"I thought Roger was your best friend," his mother said.

"Nope. Not anymore. It's Bull and Fergie now. Fergie and Bull – we're a team. He's the greatest! Mom, he told the funniest story at lunch today about a caterpillar and a crocodile."

In Fergie's eyes, Bull Frog could do no wrong. He was the best frog in the whole swamp. Fergie did everything with Bull – until the day that Bull met a girl frog.

That day Fergie came home early for supper.

"Where's Bull?" asked Mother Frog. "Isn't he coming for supper? I made extra macaroni and bees."

Fergie frowned. "He's not coming. He went to Felicity Frog's place – again. That's the fourth time this week." Fergie felt sad. "I don't think Bull and I are going to be friends anymore."

"Then why don't you call Roger? He might come and stay over tonight," suggested Father Frog.

"Good idea," said Fergie. Then he gulped, "I hope Roger will still be my friend."

Sure enough, Roger came for supper that night. The two old friends played hide-and-seek until the moon rose.

"Thanks for coming over," said Fergie as the two frogs snuggled into the mud. "Sorry I was so dumb to spend all my time with Bull Frog lately. Still friends?" Fergie asked Roger.

"Sure," said Roger. "I always knew you were dumb, Fergie. That's why you're my best friend." Roger smiled as Fergie poked him.

"Same old Fergie," said Roger.

"Same old Roger," Fergie said with a yawn.

And the two little frogs sank into the mud and went to sleep.

Reflecting on the story

When a friend stops being a friend, it hurts deep down inside. The best friends are friends who will be there for us whenever we need them. That's the kind of friend Jesus is. That's the kind of friend we can be for someone else – with Jesus' love inside us.

Talking about the story

- Can you think of a time when something a friend did made you sad?
- How do you feel if one of your friends finds a new friend?
- What makes someone a good friend? What makes you a good friend?

Praying after the story

Jesus, thank you for being there whenever I need you. When a friend lets me down and I feel lonely, touch me with your love. Make me a good friend to my friends so that we can be there for each other. Amen.

Prince Fergie?

Faith theme:
Jesus shows us God's love. We are special to God.

One afternoon at school, Ms. Nimbleknees read the story of *The Frog Prince* to Fergie the Frog's class. Fergie was very excited.

"Imagine," he said to his best friend, Roger, as they hopped home from school, "all you have to do is find a princess to kiss you and POOF!

You can live in a castle and have all the gnat burgers and french flies you want!"

"Kiss a princess? Gross!" said Roger. "Besides, how do you know you can get gnat burgers in a castle?"

"When you're a prince, you can have anything you want. That's the way it works," said Fergie. He had it all figured out. "Prince Ferguson of the Forest. That's me! You can be Sir Roger the Swampface," Fergie laughed. "Now all I have to do is find a princess."

"And get her to kiss you!" Sir Roger reminded him. "Let's see who is the Swampface!"

The swamp was running short of princesses that year. First, Fergie found Cindy the Sandpiper hunting for grubs. "Cindy," he asked, "would you kiss me?"

Cindy choked on her grub. "Kiss a frog? Why?"

Fergie explained that he was looking for a princess and that Cindy seemed like a really royal bird. Cindy smiled while Fergie closed his eyes and held his breath. Cindy pecked him on the nose.

Fergie opened one eye. All he could see were his own webbed toes. He sighed. "Better luck next princess. Thanks anyway, Cindy."

On Fergie hopped until he came across Margie Muskrat. "Margie, you are the most majestic muskrat in the swamp," he began.

"Fergie," interrupted Margie, "are you selling Frog Scout cookies again?"

"No, no," said Fergie, "I'm trying to find a princess to kiss me and turn me into a prince."

When Margie Muskrat stopped laughing, she bent over Fergie and nuzzled him with her nose and whiskers. Smack! "When you find your castle, Fergie, can I come and swim in the bathtubs?" Margie giggled.

Fergie blushed bright green. "Laugh all you want, Margie, but you just wait until I'm Prince of this place! You'll see!" As Fergie hopped away, Margie slapped her tail on the ground, laughing.

At last Fergie found Tanya the Turtle resting on the path. "Tanya! I need your help in a scientific experiment," Fergie explained, trying to sound very official. "I am testing the power of the kiss to make wishes come true."

"Okay, Fergie, I heard you. You want to become a prince. Pucker up and let's see what the Queen of the Swamp can do for you!" Tanya poked her head way out of her shell.

Very gently, very slowly, Fergie brought his lips up to meet Tanya's. He held his breath for a split second as frog and turtle touched.

"I hope I don't get warts on my lips," said Tanya, breaking the spell.

Fergie's eyes popped open. No crown. No sword. No prince.

"I guess I need a real princess," he thought sadly as he hopped home for supper.

As the Frog family gathered at the round rock table that evening, Fergie told the story of the Frog Prince and how he had tried to become a prince. He was very disappointed that he was still just a frog.

"How come three kisses couldn't turn me into a prince?" he asked.

His father shrugged and said, "Wishes don't always come true, Fergie. Maybe there isn't a prince inside you."

"Look on the bright side," said his mother. "If you were a prince, you couldn't sleep in the mud or eat this mushroom pizza with double fleas."

"Swell," said Fergie. He took a big bite of pizza. But in his heart of hearts he wondered why he couldn't be a prince and have his pizza, too.

Reflecting on the story

At Christmas, we call Jesus the Prince of Peace, but he wasn't born in a castle. Sometimes we call Jesus Lord and King, but he lived in an ordinary town and ate with his friends in their homes. Jesus lived an ordinary life, just like we do, to show us just how much God cares for ordinary people like us!

Talking about the story

- What do you think it would be like to be a prince or a princess?
- Is there anything about yourself that you would change if you could? Why?
- What do you enjoy most about your life right now? What do you like about yourself right now? Say a prayer to give thanks for all those things!

Praying after the story

Lord Jesus, Prince of Peace, thank you for loving ordinary people. Help me to feel special, even though I don't live in a castle. Help me to feel special because you love me – just the way I am. Amen.

Fergie Learns a Lesson

Faith theme:
God guides us to keep us safe.

Life situation:
Breaking rules

Feelings:
Frustration and temptation

The swamp had just begun to freeze for the winter. A thin layer of ice coated the shallow place around the bulrushes. The little frogs loved this time of year. It was so much fun to play leapfrog on new ice. Every time someone landed, they left new froggie footprints on the soft crystal crust. When someone hopped, everyone else jiggled up and down as the ice rippled.

Yes, everyone loved freeze-up time in the swamp. Everyone, that is, except Fergie the Frog. Fergie was unhappy because he was not allowed to play leapfrog on the new ice.

"It's much too dangerous," said Mother Frog.

"You might break through the ice and freeze in the water," warned Fergie's father.

Each afternoon while his friends played on the ice, Fergie had to sit on the bank and watch.

"Come on, Fergie!" shouted Roger. "This is fun. There's room for one more jumper."

"Sorry," called Fergie. "I'm not allowed on thin ice."

The other frogs giggled. "Are you afraid of freezing your tail off, Fergie?"

The games went on while Fergie sat on the bank, feeling miserable.

"Why should I miss all the fun?" Fergie thought to himself. "Everybody else can play on the ice." All at once Fergie made up his mind. "Here I come!" he yelled. He took a flying leap onto the ice.

As soon as he landed, Fergie knew something was wrong. The new ice crackled. His back feet felt the sting of icy water.

"Help!" cried Fergie. As he grabbed at the ice to pull himself out of the water, the ice crumbled into splinters. "I'm freezing! Save me!"

When the other frogs heard the ice snap, they headed for shore. Roger broke off a dried bulrush. Another frog helped him poke it across the icy water to Fergie. Fergie grabbed the bulrush and his friends hauled him to shore.

"Ohhh," he moaned. "My legs are so cold they can hardly bend. And look! I'm turning blue!"

When that little frozen frog hobbled home, Mother and Father Frog were very angry. His mother made him cattail soup, but she didn't say a word to Fergie as he sat shivering in the kitchen.

"You were a very foolish frog today, Ferguson," said Father Frog sternly. "We warned you that new ice was dangerous. You are very lucky we frogs are cold-blooded. Otherwise you might be an ice cube right now."

Fergie nodded. "I know I did a stupid thing. I'm sorry."

As he rubbed his legs to get warm, Fergie wondered why so many things that are so much fun can get a little frog into so much trouble.

Reflecting on the story

Sometimes it seems like grown-ups are always telling kids what not to do. Parents tell us. Teachers tell us. In church, we hear that God gave us laws to obey. Sometimes rules make us think we're missing out on fun. But God's rules are made to keep us safe, to keep us from hurting ourselves and from hurting each other.

Talking about the story

- Name a few rules that keep you from getting hurt.
- What happens if you break a rule? How do you feel when you break a rule and something goes wrong?
- Are there any rules you follow as a family that you don't like? Talk about why you have those rules.

Praying after the story

Dear God,

Show me how to live safely and wisely in your world. When we are having fun, keep us safe. Help us understand how rules keep us from getting hurt and from hurting others. Amen.

Fergie Loses a Friend

The ice had melted in the swamp and all the little frogs were excited. It was water polo season at last! Every day after school, the frogs practised swimming with the ball and hitting it with their noses.

Fergie the Frog loved water polo. One Saturday as he set off for practice, his father said, "Be careful, Fergie. Remember that when spring comes, humans like to catch frogs in the swamp."

Fergie shuddered, "Do you suppose humans put us in sandwiches to eat?"

"I don't know," replied Father Frog. "No frog I know has ever escaped from human hands. So just be careful today."

When Fergie arrived at the water polo pool, the practice had already started. Hoppy was the goalie. He had the strongest legs of all the little frogs. He could jump very high and catch the water polo ball in his mouth. Nobody could get that ball past Hoppy.

The water was quite cold and Fergie had to swim fast to keep warm. As he was swimming underwater, he saw the ball land PLOP! right above him. Fergie burst out of the water and hit the ball with his nose so hard it flew over Hoppy's head, sailed over the goal and landed on the shore.

"What a shot!" yelled Hoppy. "I'll get it," he called as he headed towards the grass where the ball lay.

"Great nose, Fergie!" the little frogs exclaimed. "You'll make the team for sure!"

Faith theme:
God is with us at sad times. Jesus' tears are God's tears.

Life situation:
Someone we care about leaves or dies

Feelings:
Sadness

Christian Year Connection:
Lent

Fergie wiggled his nose. It still hurt a bit.

Suddenly, a noise from the shore made him blink. A frog croaked, "Humans!"

"Dive!" yelled Fergie, who could see children moving through the grass.

Every frog sank into the water right away. Some hid in the reeds; others wiggled into the mud. Fergie held his breath underwater for as long as he could.

When he finally came up for air, everything was quiet. Fergie looked around carefully. He couldn't see any children hiding. One by one, the other little frogs appeared.

"Where's the ball?" asked Diver. "Did the humans find it?"

"Where's Hoppy?" asked Fergie, counting noses. "Hoppy! Hoppy!" they called.

There was no answer. Hoppy was gone.

"The humans caught him! What shall we do?" cried Fergie.

But there was nothing they could do.

That night at supper, Fergie was very sad. He couldn't eat his flyburger. He wouldn't even touch his mud ripple ice cream.

"What will we do without Hoppy? He was our very best goalie. Do you think he'll ever come back, Dad?" Fergie asked.

His father looked Fergie straight in the eyes. "I hope so, Fergie, but you will have to be brave. No frog captured by humans has ever come back to the swamp."

Fergie was very, very sad. He was so sad, he cried himself to sleep that night. He knew deep inside that he would never see Hoppy again.

Reflecting on the story

Sometimes very sad things happen in the world. People we love get sick or move away. People die and their friends miss them very much.

Our sad times make God sad, too. Jesus cried when his friend Lazarus died. Whenever we feel sad is a good time to pray. When we pray, we come very close to God, who will wipe away our tears.

Talking about the story

- Talk about a time when you felt very sad. What happened?
- What helps you feel better when you're feeling sad and lonely?
- Think about special people or special animals you miss. Say a prayer of thanks to God that they are still special to you.

Praying after the story

Dear God,

I wish that sad things would never happen. When I feel sad, help me remember that you are near. Your love is stronger than all the things that make me sad. Help me feel your love whenever I feel like crying. Amen.

Fergie Goes Moose Hunting

Faith theme:
We can't see God;
we see God's love
at work.

Life situation:
Looking
for something
we haven't seen

Feelings:
Uncertainty

Rumour had it there was a moose loose in the swamp. Fergie the Frog had never seen a moose in all of his seven summers. He didn't even know what a moose looked like. Fergie asked his big brother, Freddie, "Is a moose bigger than a raccoon?"

"Oh, yes," said Freddie, "*much* bigger. Even bigger than that deer we saw nibbling grass near the swamp last fall."

"You're kidding!" cried Fergie, with his eyes bugging out of his head. "That deer was the biggest thing I ever saw. Have you ever seen a real moose, Freddie?"

Freddie shook his head. "No, but I saw a picture at school once. They look mean and ugly."

"I'd like to see a real live moose," Fergie went on. "If there is one in the swamp, why don't we go find it?"

"Okay," said Freddie. "Let's pack a lunch and go moose hunting this afternoon."

The two little frogs made some peanut butter and fly sandwiches and grabbed two bottles of swamp soda. They stuffed their food into a backpack and hopped off to find a moose.

First, they headed to the north end of the swamp, where some birds had seen the moose. The birds had disappeared, but Margie the Muskrat was sitting there on the muddy shore, chewing on some roots.

"Margie, have you seen the moose today?" Fergie called.

"No, not today. It's gone. But look! You can see its tracks."

Sure enough, huge hoofprints big enough for Freddie and Fergie to sit in together led away from the swamp. "Let's follow them," suggested Freddie. The hoofprints led towards the marsh.

At the edge of the marsh, Ernie the Porcupine was gnawing on a broken tree. "Ernie! Where's the moose?" Fergie asked. "We're hunting moose today."

Ernie looked up. "What would you do if you found a moose, Fergie? It did come this way. It broke this little tree and crushed the marsh grass as it ran. Something must have scared it. Was it running away from you?" Ernie chuckled.

"We'll find it, Ernie," Fergie declared. Off the two frogs headed through the thick marsh grass, hot on the moose's trail.

When they reached the forest, Rachel the Robin whistled at them. "Where are you hopping in such a hurry?" she asked.

"We're moose hunting," said Fergie. "Which way did it go?"

Rachel cocked her head and looked around. Just then, a booming bellow split the silence of the forest.

"Gee, that sounded like a giant bullfrog with an upset stomach!" Fergie exclaimed.

"Sounds like the bullfrog exploded," Freddie gulped.

"No, no," said Rachel Robin. "That was a moose call. Follow that sound and you'll find your moose."

But by then it was time to go home for supper. Fergie was disappointed they had missed the moose. He wondered if Freddie and the other animals were trying to fool him. How could any animal have feet so big? Or break off little trees? Or hurt your eardrums just by bellowing?

At supper, Fergie announced that he didn't believe there was a moose in the swamp.

"I want to see one with my very own eyes before I believe there is such a thing as a moose. I think Freddie took me on a wild moose chase today!"

Reflecting on the story

It is hard to believe in something we haven't seen for ourselves. Sometimes it's hard to believe in God when we can't see God's face or touch God's hand. But all around us there are signs of God's work.

Just like Fergie could see signs of where the moose had been, and how powerful it was, we can see signs of God at work in the world. Wherever we see love change people's lives, whenever people stop to help a stranger or care for someone in need, there is a sign of God's power working in our lives.

Talking about the story

- Even though we can't see God, Jesus shows us how God's love works in people's lives. Name some things Jesus did to show us God's love.
- Where have you seen people helping each other as a sign of God's love?

- How can you show God's love by what you do?

Praying after the story

Dear God,

Help us to hunt for signs of your love in our lives, in our church, and in the world. Whenever we wonder where you are, whenever we need you, touch us with your Spirit and show us the way to go – the way of Jesus. Amen.

Fergie Cleans Up

One summer day, some human campers pitched a tent near the stream that led into the swamp. Fergie the Frog was very excited. He had never seen people so close before. Fergie and his brother, Freddie, watched them with interest. The campers hung their food in a tree so animals couldn't eat it. They put bottles in the stream to keep their drinks cool.

"Do you suppose they sleep in the mud?" asked Fergie.

"No," said Freddie. "They probably sleep in trees, like raccoons. Then the bears won't eat them – or their food."

The next morning, Fergie woke up to find his mud hole covered in white bubbles. "Hey! What's this?" he asked.

"Camper fizz," said his mother. "The humans threw their dishwater in the stream. Now this foam is all over the swamp."

Fergie made a face. "Ick!"

Faith theme:
We can care for God's world.

Life situation:
People making a mess for others to clean up

Feelings:
Concern, resentment

165

At supper it got worse. The campers walked to the swamp and dumped the charcoal from their barbecue into the Frogs' living room. "It won't start a fire here," one of them said.

"What do you mean?" yelled Fergie. "It could start a fire in my bed! Do you want roast frog for breakfast?" He was hopping mad – so mad he hopped on a piece of charcoal and sizzled his foot. "Ouch!" he croaked.

"Listen to the frogs, Jane," said another camper. "Isn't it great to be away from the city noise?"

The Frogs decided they would move until their house cooled off. They went off in different directions to look for safe places to hide. Fergie was in some tall reeds not very far from the stream when it happened.

The campers dumped their garbage. They dumped their garbage into the tall grass, right on top of Fergie.

"Hey, watch out!" he croaked.

Then CLUNK! A big glass pop bottle fell right on top of Fergie and knocked him out.

Two hours later, the search party found him.

"Ohhhh!" Fergie groaned. He couldn't move – the bottle had pinned his legs to the ground.

"Fergie!" cried Mother Frog. "Are you all right?"

He moaned again. "I can't move my legs. I think they're broken."

The whole Frog family pushed on the bottle until it rolled away. Then they carried Fergie to a safer place between the roots of a tree.

As his mother bandaged his legs, Fergie asked, "Were those campers trying to kill me?"

"No, Fergie, I don't think so," she said. "They just never thought about you." She shook her head sadly. "They just never thought."

Reflecting on the story

For a long time, people just never thought about looking after animals and streams and trees and fresh air. We were like the campers in the story, dumping our garbage wherever we liked, never stopping to think that it might hurt the plants and animals. Now we know that unless we are more careful, the things we do and the way we live can hurt the earth.

God made human beings to look after the earth and take care of all the beautiful plants and animals. So stop and think. Make sure what you do is not hurting anything God made.

Talking about the story

- What are some ways that people make a mess in the world or hurt other creatures?
- What can campers do to take care of God's world when they are camping?
- What can we do to take care of the world?

Praying after the story

Dear God,

You made the beautiful butterfly and the funny frog. You made the gentle breeze and the roaring ocean. Help us look after all these beautiful things. Make us stop and think so that we can live together safely in your world. Amen.

Fergie Gets a Surprise

Author's note: This is a three-part story designed to be used in a single worship service around the start of a new school year. Each story can also be used on a separate occasion.

Part 1 – What About Fergie?

Faith theme:
We belong to God.
We are special
to God.

Life situation:
When someone new
arrives in our family

Feelings:
Jealousy

Fergie and his big brother, Freddie, were sitting on a rock, trying to catch the first mosquitoes. Freddie's tongue was a little longer, so he was catching a few more.

"I wish my tongue was longer!" Fergie complained.

Freddie grinned. "Let's tie a rock to the tip of your tongue to see if it will stretch."

Just then Father Frog appeared. "I've got some good news for you!" he said.

Fergie perked up. "Is Mom making poached roach for supper tonight?"

"Nope! Your mother's down at the tad pool," his father said.

"Babysitting for Aunt Tilly?" asked Freddie.

Father Frog shook his head and smiled. "She's feeding your new baby sister, Fiona!"

Fergie frowned. "A sister? We didn't ask for a sister, Dad. We wanted scooters."

"You'll really like Fiona," said Father. "She has the longest tail a tad ever had. She's going to be a jumper. Now I'll go heat up the macaroni and fleas for supper. Then we'll go see Fiona and your mom."

When his father hopped away, Fergie made a face. "We had macaroni and fleas last night. And the night before."

Freddie nodded. "That's what happens when a new tadpole arrives. When you were born, Fergie, I had macaroni and fleas for a month. That's how Dad cooks."

Fergie sighed. "If Fiona has the longest tail in the family, and you have the longest tongue, what about me? You'll still be the biggest and the oldest. Now Fiona will be the smallest and the youngest. Who will I be?"

Just then Father Frog called, "Fergie! Freddie! Supper's ready!"

Freddie said, "I know who you can be, Fergie. You really like to eat. Maybe you can be the best cook in the family. Then we won't have to eat macaroni and fleas anymore!"

Reflecting on the story

Whenever a new school year begins, we know we're going to meet somebody new. Maybe it won't be our very own baby sister, but there will be someone new in our class or on our team or at church. Meeting somebody new changes the world for all of us. That can be a little scary until we figure out how we fit with someone new and how all of us, old and new, fit together in God's world. Always remember that God has a special place for you!

Talking about the story

- Remember a time when someone new joined your class or your family. How did you feel?
- Have you ever been new in a place where everyone else knew each other? How did you feel? Who made you feel welcome?

Praying after the story

God, you have made a place for each one of us in your world. When I meet someone new, show me your face in his face and her face. Help us make a place for each other in our lives. Amen.

Part 2 – Fergie and Fiona

The second part of the story happened later that summer...

One afternoon, it was Fergie's turn to carry the mosquito mush down to the tad pool. Freddie was feeding Fiona while their parents hunted for more mosquitoes.

"Glad you brought that mush, Fergie," Freddie said. "She sure eats a lot for a little tad."

Fiona wiggled her tail and said, "Bibbit, bibbit."

Fergie looked at Fiona and shook his head. "I wonder if she'll ever turn into a real frog. She's got those little legs now, but how will she ever hop with that tail? Dad says she'll be a jumper but all she does is eat and wiggle. Do you suppose she'll ever be any fun?"

Fiona wiggled her tail and said, "Feedee. Feedee."

Freddie shrugged and said, "She just keeps asking me to feed her."

Fergie laughed. "No way. That's your name. Fee-dee the frog. Ha, ha, ha. That's what I'll call you from now on. My big brother Feedee."

As Freddie zapped Fergie in the head with his tongue, Fiona wiggled her tail and said, "Feed me, Feedee."

"It's your turn to feed her, Fergie. I have to go to diving practice." And away hopped Freddie.

"BYE, FEEDEE!" yelled Fergie.

Then Fergie looked at Fiona. "You're a phony frog, Fiona. You don't belong in this family."

Fiona wiggled her tail and said, "Phonee Feegoo. Phonee Feegoo."

Fergie held out a spoonful of mosquito mush. "Okay. Okay. Here's your goo."

"Feegoo," said Fiona.

A voice chuckled behind him. It was his grandmother. "She's saying your name, Fergie. Feegoo. That's you."

Fergie gulped. "You're kidding, Grandma. Don't tell Freddie. I'll be Feegoo forever!"

"Feegoo," said Fiona again.

"Shhhh," Fergie said.

"She likes you, Fergie. That's why she calls you," said Grandma.

"But Grandma," said Fergie, "she's no fun. We don't need her in this family. She can't catch mosquitoes. She can't play leapfrog. She can't even talk right."

"Phonee Gamma, Feegoo," said Fiona, wiggling her tail.

"Ah, she'll be a jumper someday. You'll see," said Grandma. "Give her time."

"Feegoo! Feegoo!" Fiona said with a smile.

Fergie looked at his sister and shook his head again. "I really wanted a scooter!" he said softly.

Reflecting on the story

Everyone in our family is a little bit different from the others. Everyone in the world is a little bit different from every other person. Sometimes what is different about another person seems weird. But really what seems different about someone else is God's gift to us. God invites us to learn something from everyone who is different from us. And that makes God's world a very interesting place!

Talking about the story

- Think about the people in your family. How are your family members alike?
- How is each person different from everyone else?

Praying after the story

God, you make each one of us a little different from the others. You make each of us special in some way. Help us learn from each other and with each other this year, so that we discover the gifts you give us in each other. Amen.

Part 3 – Fergie Changes His Mind

The last part of the story happens in the fall of that year, when Fiona is four months old...

One warm September afternoon, Grandma Frog was snoozing beside the tad pool. Fergie arrived carrying a jar of stewed worms. "Wake up, Grandma. Time to feed that little monster mouth again!"

Grandma Frog blinked. "Hi, Fergie. You know, I think it's time to take Fiona home to the swamp. She's eating enough to feed a herd of horseflies."

"Grandma, she could eat a horsefly by herself if we let her."

They looked into the pool.

"Oh no! Fiona's gone!" cried Fergie. "Somebody stole my sister!"

"Yoo-hoo! Feegoo!" a little voice called.

Fergie and Grandma looked around. There sat Fiona on top of a big rock beside the tad pool. "Phonee jump!" she said.

"You *are* a great little jumper, Fiona!" said Grandma. "Let's go home."

"Come down, Fiona," said Fergie. "Time to go."

"Phonee no jump," said Fiona. She just sat there.

Grandma chuckled. "She can jump up, Fergie, but she can't jump down yet. We'll have to show her how."

So Grandma Frog jumped up on the rock and then jumped down.

"Gamma jump," said Fiona. "Phonee no jump."

Fergie thought for minute. "Grandma, I've got an idea. Let's both hop on the rock."

So they did.

Then Fergie said, "Grandma, you jump down first. Then I'll jump on your back. Fiona can jump on me. We'll make a frog pyramid, just like we do at school."

So Grandma Frog jumped to the ground. Then Fergie hopped onto her back.

"Ugh!" shivered Grandma. "You have cold feet!"

Fergie called, "Fiona! Jump on my back. You can do it."

Fiona blinked. She made a tiny hop to the edge of the rock. She blinked again.

"Come on, Phonee. You can jump!"

And then she did. She landed right on Fergie's head. "Phonee jump!" she said proudly.

"Now we both jump!" said Fergie. He hopped off Grandma's back onto the ground.

Then Fiona jumped and landed on the path.

Grandma Frog smiled. "That's my little jumper! We'll teach you how to play leapfrog on the way home."

"Eepfog?" asked Fiona.

"Right!" said Fergie. "Eepfog. Our favourite family game."

Fergie jumped over Fiona. Then Fiona jumped over Fergie. Grandma Frog sailed over both of them.

"Wheeee! Gamma jump," said Fiona. Then she jumped over Grandma Frog.

"My sister *is* a great little jumper!" thought Fergie. "She might just be more fun than a scooter after all!"

Reflecting on the story

We're all different from each other and we all have something special to bring to God's family. No matter who we are and what we can do for ourselves, we still need each other. Sometimes we help each other. Sometimes we figure things out together. When we work and play together, we bring joy to God and to God's world.

Talking about the story

- Name something special about each person in your family – including yourself.
- What are some of the things the people in your family do to help each other?
- How do you have fun together?

Praying after the story

Thank you, God, for my family, for brothers and sisters, parents and children, grandparents, our aunts and uncles and cousins. You made each person special in some way. Show me how I am special to you and to other people. Let me bring joy to you and to the world for Jesus' sake. Amen.

Presenting Sherman the Hound Dog

Treasure Hunt

"Hey, Sherman!" called Mark. "Do you want to go on a treasure hunt?"

Sherman was sleeping on the step. He opened one eye. "Treasure hunt? Where are we going? To the dump or to the mall?"

"No, no," said Lucy. "We're just going to the vacant lot. Mark heard that people bury things there sometimes."

"Like steak bones?" asked Sherman.

"Maybe," said Mark. "But we hope we might find some money or some jewellery. You know, real treasure!"

Sherman thought for a minute. "I don't know. A steak bone is worth more to me than earrings. But I guess I'll come. Maybe somebody buried a steak bone with some money to buy a new steak."

So Mark and Lucy and Sherman set out for the vacant lot. Mark had a big shovel and Lucy pulled the wagon.

"Just in case we find a treasure chest that is too big to carry," she said, grinning.

When they reached the lot, Mark said, "Okay, Sherman, you are our treasure hound. Start sniffing. Tell us when you smell treasure."

"Yeah," said Lucy, "real treasure, not just steak bones."

Sherman put his nose to the ground. SNIFFFF! "Smells like dirt to me. No treasure here."

"Keep going," urged Lucy. "How about sniffing out those big rocks? Maybe the rocks mark the spot where pirates buried their treasure."

Faith theme:
God loves us.
We are special
to God.

Life situation:
Hunting
for "treasure"

Feelings:
Curiosity and
excitement

177

Sherman sniffed the rocks. "What does treasure smell like? This just smells like something cold and hard."

"Let's dig anyway," said Mark. "Maybe you're smelling a cold, hard treasure chest underneath these rocks!"

Mark started digging with the shovel. Lucy pulled the rocks away from the hole. They dug and they dug.

Sherman got a little bored just watching. "Think I'll check out that tree." He sniffed his way over to the tree. "Gee, I really smell something here! Not a steak bone. Looks like somebody's been digging, too!"

The earth was soft where Sherman started to dig. As he dug, the smell got better and better.

"I found the treasure!" he barked. Lucy and Mark came running. "Look! There *is* something buried here."

"Let me dig it out," said Mark. "Stand back." In a couple of minutes, Mark pulled out a gym bag. "Great! Maybe we'll find some money inside."

"Be careful," said Lucy. "Maybe this bag is full of stolen jewels."

Slowly Mark opened the zipper. Then he made a face. "Phew! This smells awful."

He dumped the bag on the ground. Out fell a pair of sneakers and some dirty socks. There was a lunch bag filled with rotting leftovers. "Ugh!" coughed Mark.

"Ick!" said Lucy. "Put it back in the hole."

"No way," said Sherman. "This is my treasure. I found it. Finders keepers, losers weepers. I love sneakers and dirty socks."

Sherman grabbed a sneaker and gave it a good hard shake. Then he sniffed the socks and tossed one up in the air.

"Yum!" he said. "A dirty sock is almost as good as a steak bone!"

Reflecting on the story

If you were hunting for treasure, what would you look for? Gold? Jewels? Money? Where would you look for treasure? In a faraway land? Or in your own backyard? Treasure means different things to different people. For God, *we* are a treasure. Each one of us is very special to God. So always remember that you are the treasure that God loves!

Talking about the story

- What kind of treasure would you like to find? Where would you look?
- Sometimes we talk about special people as treasures. Who are some people that are special to you? What makes them special?
- What's special about you?

Praying after the story

Dear God,

It makes me glad to know that you love me. Help me see what is special about my life, and help me find the treasure you have found in the people around me. Amen.

Name Blame

Sherman was sitting in the backyard, chained to the picnic table.

"I wonder when Claude the Cat will show his furry face?" Sherman said to himself.

He didn't have long to wait. The bushes near the fence rustled. Suddenly Claude, the cat who lived next door, jumped on top of the fence.

"Miaow, Bonebreath!" said Claude. Then he hissed at Sherman.

Sherman knew the game. "Get off my fence, Liverlips," he barked.

Sherman barked and he barked. He ran at the fence until his chain pulled him back. Claude spit and arched his back. Then he disappeared.

Just then Mark appeared. "Sherman, don't be so stupid. You can't get Claude. You're chained up."

Sherman calmed down, so Mark let him loose.

"I'm not stupid. I was just playing the game the way we always play the game," Sherman thought to himself. He didn't like being called stupid, so he sat under the table and sulked.

While he was sulking, Max, the little terrier from two houses over, stuck his head underneath the back fence. "Hey, Tubby," he called to Sherman, "let's play tag!"

"You rat!" barked Sherman. How he hated being called Tubby, especially by that runt of a dog. So Sherman chased Max around and around the yard.

Then Max squeezed underneath the fence again.

"Ha, ha, ha, Tubby," Max yapped. "Can't catch me for a bumblebee."

"I'll show you!" Sherman began to dig furiously in the garden by the fence. "I can make this hole big enough for me, too."

No sooner had Sherman begun to dig when a deep voice yelled, "Sherman! You idiot! How many times have I told you not to dig in the garden!" Father yanked Sherman's collar and hauled him out of the flowers. He slapped Sherman's dirty nose. "Bad dog!"

Sherman slunk inside the house. He was grumpy.

"What a rotten day. Claude calls me Bonebreath. Mark calls me stupid. Max calls me Tubby. Then Father calls me an idiot."

Sherman hid under Lucy's bed. He didn't even come out for supper. He wouldn't chase the ball when Lucy threw it for him. He just lay under the bed, feeling miserable.

At last Lucy crawled under the bed, too.

"What's wrong, you silly old dog? You missed supper. Why won't you come out?" she asked.

"Don't call me a silly old dog. I'm staying under here until I find a new name. How about Lassie? Or Snoopy? I want a name that makes me feel better. And silly old dog won't do."

"I'm sorry, Sherman. I was only teasing," said Lucy. "How about if I call you one more time for supper tonight? Maybe you'll feel better if you have dinner. Come on. Let's go find some chow."

"I guess you can *always* call me for supper," Sherman said with a wag of his tail.

Reflecting on the story

Words are very powerful. Words can hurt people or words can make people feel better. If somebody calls you by a name that hurts, remember that God knows your real name. God calls you by your own name because God loves you.

Talking about the story

- How do you feel when somebody calls you names?
- Are there any names you really don't like to be called?
- What name do you like people to call you? What's important about that name to you?
- Jesus taught us the Golden Rule: "In everything, do to others what you would like them to do to you." How does this help you think if you are tempted to call someone names?

Praying after the story

Dear God,

I remember times when somebody called me a name that hurt me inside. I remember times when I called somebody a name because I was mad. Help me use words to make people feel better. Call me by my own name and remind me that you love me in Jesus' name. Amen.

It's Good for You

"Sherman, do you want some mashed potatoes?" Lucy whispered at supper the day after New Year's.

Sherman lay behind her chair. "No, thanks, Lucy. I'm not hungry tonight." Poor Sherman didn't feel well.

"Mom," said Lucy. "I think something is wrong with Sherman."

"What makes you think so?"

"He didn't want to watch the Dalmatians movie on TV tonight. And now he won't eat my mashed potatoes," Lucy said.

"And we all know Sherman likes mashed potatoes better than Lucy does," Mark teased. "Maybe Sherman is just tired of reruns," Mark added, "of TV *and* mashed potatoes."

As Sherman groaned, Father said, "I guess we'd better take him to the doctor tomorrow."

The next morning Sherman went to the veterinarian's. The doctor kept him for a whole day – for tests.

Sherman sighed, "I'm too tired to take tests."

When Lucy came to take him home, Sherman said, "I'm sure glad to see you. Hospital food is terrible."

The doctor said, "I think Sherman must have eaten some garbage. Give him this medicine three times a day with a vitamin. No cookies or sweet things. He needs to build up his strength."

"Sherman," Lucy asked on the way home in the car, "did you eat some garbage?"

Faith theme:
God is always with us.

Life situation:
Being sick

Feelings:
Unhappiness

Sherman shook his head. "I never eat garbage. Leftovers maybe, but not garbage. Like the bag of leftover turkey I found in the lane. Turkey isn't garbage – so I ate it."

"That's what made you sick," Lucy said. "Rotten turkey. Now you have to eat this." Lucy squirted the medicine in Sherman's mouth.

"Argh! Lucy, that medicine tastes rotten. It will make me sicker!" Sherman tried to lick the medicine off his tongue.

"Get used to it! The doctor said three times a day for ten days," Lucy said.

"Couldn't we share it, Lucy, like your mashed potatoes?" asked Sherman.

They tried everything to make the medicine taste better. First they tried water to wash it down. "Water's not strong enough. I need hot chocolate," said Sherman.

"Here," said Mark. "Try this cracker."

"Couldn't I have a cookie instead?" Sherman asked.

"The doctor said no cookies till you're stronger," Lucy explained.

"Then how about some peppermints to give me some pep? Did the Doctor mention candy?" Sherman wagged his tail.

"The doctor said no sweet things till you're better," Mark insisted. "So eat this cracker."

"Thanks a lot. I'll turn into a sourpuss before this medicine is gone!" Sherman complained as he nibbled the cracker. "I still feel as crummy as this cracker."

Reflecting on the story

Some things that are good for us don't taste good. Sometimes the medicine to make us feel better tastes awful. Whenever you have to take medicine or do something important that isn't easy or fun, remember that God is with you. When we're sick or having a hard time, God helps us make it through.

Talking about the story

- Name something that's good for you but tastes bad to you.
- Remember a time when you were sick and had to stay home. What happened?
- What kinds of things help you feel better when you're sick?

Praying after the story

Dear God,

Whenever I'm sick, whenever I'm having a hard time, come and be with me. Show me your love. Help me grow stronger day by day. Amen.

When Sleeping Dogs Lie

"Hey, Sherman!" called Lucy. "I'm going to the library. Want to come? We could get ice cream on the way home."

Sherman was lying on the couch. "No, thanks, Lucy. I'm not hungry."

"Sherman, are you sick? You never turn down ice cream," Lucy said.

Faith theme:
God forgives us. We can set things right.

Life situation:
Telling a lie

185

Feelings:
Worry, shame

"I'm okay, Lucy," said Sherman. "I don't have any books to take back anyway. I ate my last one last week. I'm going to the park with Mark."

Lucy shrugged. "See you later." Sherman closed his eyes.

A few minutes later, Mark called, "Sherman, want to come to the park and play Frisbee?"

"No, thanks, Mark," Sherman said with his eyes still closed. "I'm watching TV."

"You are not. You have your eyes closed," Mark said.

"Father watches TV with his eyes closed every night," Sherman reminded him.

"Come on, Sherman," Mark urged. "I can't play Frisbee by myself."

"Sorry. I promised Lucy I'd go to the library with her this afternoon," Sherman explained.

Mark shook his head. "You'd pick the library over the park? You must have dog pox. Suit yourself. I'll find someone else to play with." Mark banged the door as he left.

Sherman lay on the couch. "I wish I did have the dog pox. Then I wouldn't have to go outside ever again."

When Lucy was coming home from the library, she met Mark carrying his Frisbee. "Where's Sherman?" she asked. "He said he was going to play with you."

Mark shrugged, "He told me he was going to the library with you." The children stared at each other.

"Let's go get him!" Lucy cried.

When the door banged, Sherman opened one eye. "There he is!" Mark shouted.

"Sherman, you bag of bones. You lied to us. Why won't you come outside?" Lucy demanded.

"I'm allergic to fresh air," Sherman pouted.

"You are not," said Lucy. "You like to sleep in the sun."

"Not anymore. I might get a sunburn and then my fur would peel off. Do you want a barenaked dog?" asked Sherman.

"Sherman, you are not telling the truth. You love the park. You love sun and fresh air. What is wrong with you?" Mark asked.

"I can't go outside. Someone might take me to jail." Sherman hung his head.

Lucy's eyes opened wide. "What did you do?"

"I stole a bone from Fifi, the poodle next door. I buried it in the garden under the marigolds. There. Now you know. Now you'll have to send me to jail," Sherman said sadly.

"Sherman! *You* dug up mother's marigolds? She blamed Fifi," Mark said slowly.

"Yeah. But Fifi was only trying to get her bone back. What am I going to do now?" Sherman asked.

"You old hound dog! You"ll have to say you're sorry," Mark said.

"Apologize to Fifi? That piece of fluff?" Sherman shook his head.

"And to Mom. She's no piece of fluff," said Lucy.

"Do you think she'll send me to jail?" Sherman asked.

"I don't think so," grinned Mark.

"Yeah," said Lucy, "Mom didn't send us to jail when we wrecked her rose garden."

"You wrecked her roses? So, we're partners in crime," Sherman said with a grateful smile.

"Come on, partner," said Mark. "It's time to say you're sorry."

Reflecting on the story

When we lie about something we did, the bad feeling inside doesn't go away. We may even feel worse. If you ever feel that way, remember that God's love is still with you – even when you've done something wrong. God's love can help you set things right again!

Talking about the story

- Can you remember a time someone lied about something that happened? How did you feel?
- What makes it hard to tell the truth sometimes?
- Can you remember a time when you told the truth even though it was hard? What happened?

Praying after the story

Dear God,

You know me through and through. And you love me. Help me feel your love close by when I have to say sorry for something I did. Help me set things right again for Jesus' sake. Amen.

Temper Tantrum

"Hey, Lucy! Do you want to go play in the snow?" Sherman asked a few days after Christmas.

"No, thanks," she said. "I just fed Cuddly Wuddly Cutesie Pie and now I have to change her." As Lucy picked up her new doll, it let out a little burp and said, "Ma-ma."

Sherman wandered away, muttering, "Dumb doll." He waddled into Mark's bedroom. "Mark, will you come and play in the snow? We could build a fort to guard us from cats."

"Sorry, Sherman," said Mark. "I'm not finished putting together my model railway yet. Maybe tomorrow."

"Tomorrow?" groaned Sherman. "The snow could be gone tomorrow."

Sherman was not happy with the Christmas holidays. Mark and Lucy were busy with their new toys. The turkey leftovers were almost gone. He waddled into the den and put his paw on the TV remote. "I'll watch the soap operas. You can count on them to be there any day you want."

Sherman dozed by the TV till his stomach growled around suppertime. He sniffed. "No turkey? I wonder what's going on." Out in the hall, he found everyone putting on their coats. "Where are we going?" Sherman asked.

"We're so tired of turkey, we decided to go out for pizza and a movie," said Lucy.

Mark patted Sherman on the head. "Keep the cats out of the house, okay?" Then everyone but Sherman walked out the door.

Faith theme:
We can forgive each other and set things right.

Life situation:
Hurting somebody who has hurt us

Feelings:
Anger, frustration, being sorry

189

Sherman was mad. "We could have ordered in a pizza and rented a video. How come no one will play with me anymore?"

Sherman was so mad, he decided he would roll on all the beds. In Mark's room, he pulled the comforter right off the bed. One of Mark's train cars rolled onto the floor. "I can put the chew in choo-choo," thought Sherman. He chomped the car and left teeth marks in its roof.

Then he ran into Lucy's room. When he jumped on the bed, he found Cuddly Wuddly Cutesie Pie fast asleep. "Rock-a-bye, baby," he said. Sherman gave her a good hard shake. But as he let the doll go flying, her arm came off in his mouth. "Uh-oh," he said to himself.

Sherman knew he was in trouble. He crawled into the hall closet and hid behind the vacuum cleaner.

When the family came home after the movie, Mark whistled. "Sherman, we saved you a piece of pizza. Lots of pepperoni!" But Sherman didn't budge.

"I wonder where he is?" said Lucy. "I bet he's sleeping on my bed."

Sherman heard her come down the hall and turn on the light. Lucy let out a shriek. "A burglar pulled the arm off my doll!" She started to cry.

"It wasn't a burglar," said Mark, coming out of his room. "Look. No burglar would chew a steam engine!"

"Sherman, you bad dog! Where are you?" Lucy demanded.

No one thought to look in the hall closet. Sherman heard Lucy cry herself to sleep.

Early the next morning, he crawled out of the closet and tiptoed into Lucy's room. He jumped up and licked Lucy's face. She put her arms around him and opened one eye.

"Sherman, why did you eat Cuddly Wuddly Cutesie Pie? She was my favourite Christmas present." Lucy frowned.

"I'm sorry, Lucy. I was mad because you wouldn't play with me. But now I'm sad too. Can somebody fix her?" asked Sherman.

"Mom says we can sew her arm back on, but she won't be able to talk anymore," Lucy said sadly.

"Then maybe I could be your Cuddly Wuddly Cutesie Pie," Sherman suggested. "I can eat and burp as often as you like."

"Well, okay," said Lucy as Sherman crawled under the covers. "You're cuddlier than a doll, anyway."

"And you're much cuddlier than a vacuum cleaner," said Sherman.

Reflecting on the story

When we get left out of the fun, or when somebody makes us mad or sad, we often feel like doing something to get back at them. But hurting each other never makes things better. It just makes things worse. Jesus taught his friends to forgive each other over and over again. He asked us to treat each other the way we would like others to treat us.

Talking about the story

- Did you ever hurt somebody when you really didn't mean to?
- What did you do when that happened?
- How can you show somebody that you are sorry for what happened?

Praying after the story

Dear Jesus,

Be with me when I feel sad and when I feel mad. When I do something wrong, help me say, "I'm sorry." When someone says "Sorry" to me, help us forgive each other and be friends again. Amen.

How Big Is This Family?

Author's note: This story is somewhat longer than average, designed for a worship service in which children participate throughout. It may need editing when less than ten minutes is available.

Faith theme:
We are all part of God's family.

Life situation:
When company comes to visit

Feelings:
Jealousy, resentment

"Guess what?" asked Lucy with a frown.

"What?" asked Sherman.

"Aunt Frances is coming to visit for two weeks," Lucy said.

"So? What's wrong with Aunt Frances coming for two weeks?" Sherman wondered.

"She gets to sleep in *my* room. So I have to sleep in Mark's room – on the bottom bunk. It's not fair," Lucy pouted.

"Lucy, you sleep in the bottom bunk in your own room," Mark pointed out.

"Not all the time," she pouted. "I like the top bunk better."

Sherman thought for a minute. "If Aunt Frances gets your bed and you get the bottom bunk, then where do I sleep?"

"In the doghouse," Lucy announced.

"The doghouse? I'm not a doghouse dog," Sherman complained. "I'm a living-room-chesterfield dog. I'm a foot-of-the-bed dog. I'm not sleeping in any old doghouse. I could freeze in the middle of the night."

Lucy sighed. "I don't think you'll freeze in August, Sherman. But what we can do? Aunt Frances gets here tomorrow."

Just then Mark came in the door. "Quit complaining about Aunt Fran, Lucy. She's great. Not every kid has an aunt who's a scientist, you know."

"I know. But she's not sleeping in *your* room," Lucy pointed out.

"If Aunt Frances is a scientist, why can't she invent a way to sleep on the couch?" grumbled Sherman.

"Or in a hotel," added Lucy.

Mark shook his head. "She's Mom's sister. You don't make your *sister* sleep in a hotel. She's *family*."

"Then how come *you* make *your* sister sleep on the bottom bunk?" Lucy demanded. "*I'm* family."

"And how come you make your dog sleep in the doghouse? I'm family, too!" Sherman added.

Mark made a face at Lucy. Lucy stuck out her tongue at Mark. Then she looked at Sherman. "Maybe this family isn't big enough for you and me *and* Aunt Frances," she said. "If we don't all fit in the house, then we don't all fit in the family."

"There's room in the doghouse for both of us, Lucy. We'll be warm enough if we're together," said Sherman.

"Good idea, Sherman. Let's get my sleeping bag. We'll be our *own* family. We won't make room for anybody else," Lucy declared.

So Sherman and Lucy stuffed a sleeping bag into the doghouse along with a flashlight and a bag of chocolate cookies. "Chocolate keeps you warm, you know," said Sherman. "Now we won't freeze!"

Aunt Frances arrived the next morning. Mark carried her computer in from the car. "I'm working on a new program," she said. "Maybe you and Lucy would like to help me choose the graphics."

"Great!" said Mark.

"No, thanks," said Lucy, frowning. "I have to practise the piano," she added.

"And I have to practise howling at the piano," Sherman said.

Aunt Frances and Mark looked at each other and shook their heads.

That night after supper, Aunt Frances and Mark were busy on the computer. Lucy called Sherman. "Let's go out to the doghouse. No one will miss *us*."

They sneaked out the back door. Lucy wriggled into her sleeping bag. Sherman watched as she backed into the doghouse, feet first. Then Sherman squeezed in beside her.

"Tight squeeze, Lucy," Sherman groaned. In a few minutes, he asked, "Can you pass me a cookie, please?"

"I don't think so. I can hardly move," said Lucy.

They lay very still and waited to fall asleep. And they waited. And they waited.

At last all the lights in the house went out. A while later, the back door opened. Lucy shut her eyes when a pair of slippers appeared at her nose.

"Is there room for one more in there?" said a voice. It was Aunt Frances.

"No," said Lucy, keeping her eyes shut. "You can sleep in my bed."

"But your room has bunk beds. One of them is empty. Maybe we could have a sleepover, just the three of us," Aunt Frances suggested.

"The three of us?" asked Sherman. "In Lucy's room?"

"Sure," said Aunt Frances. "There's a place for all of us."

Sherman squirmed out of the doghouse. "C'mon, Lucy. I love you, but I don't love your sleeping bag. We'll have more room for the cookies in your room."

So the three of them tiptoed through the house. Sherman carried the bag of cookies. In Lucy's room, he jumped on to the bottom bunk and wagged his tail.

"Which bunk do you want, Lucy?" asked Aunt Frances.

"The top one!" Lucy said.

Aunt Frances gave her a hug as Lucy pulled up the covers. "Thanks for making room for me, Lucy," she said.

"And for the chocolate," said Sherman, as he munched on a cookie, "to keep us warm."

Reflecting on the story

How big is a family? Sometimes we have to make room in our family for someone new – a new brother or sister, or an aunt or uncle who comes to stay with us for a little while. Making room for someone new isn't easy. But God's love has room for everyone. So God can help us make room for someone new in our lives.

Talking about the story

- What kinds of things do you have to share in your family?
- Who shares things with you?
- How do you feel when you have to share something?

Praying after the story

Dear God,

Your love can make room for everyone. Thank you for making room for us in your family. Help us find room to share and love to spare for new people in our family. Amen.

Who's Sorry Now?

"It's my turn!" said Lucy.

"No! It's my turn," Mark said.

"You had him yesterday," Lucy pouted.

"You took him out this morning." Mark's voice was loud.

Sherman listened to the children argue. "Come on," he said. "Let's go for a walk."

"We're going to Anne's house to see her new dog," Lucy announced.

"No way," Mark yelled. "We're going to play baseball in the park." He pushed Lucy away from the door.

"Mo-om!" Lucy cried. "Mark pushed me."

Mother appeared from the kitchen. "You two! When will you learn to get along? Go to your rooms until you're ready to say you're sorry. Sherman can come to the library with me."

The children walked away scowling.

Sherman thought, "The library? I hate walks to the library. I get chained to the bike rack. And there's nothing to eat."

Then Sherman had an idea.

He wandered into Lucy's room and jumped on her bed.

"I'm sorry, Sherman," Lucy said sadly. "You would like Anne's new dog. He's a beagle hound named Sergeant."

"Lucy," Sherman said, "I think Mark wants to meet you on the front step. Maybe he's ready to say he's sorry."

Faith theme:
Jesus asks us to be peacemakers, to set things right.

Life situation:
When our friends are mad at each other

Feelings:
Uncertainty, concern

Lucy smiled. "Great. Then we can go to Anne's." She went to get her jacket.

Sherman waddled into Mark's room. "Hey, Mark. Lucy's going to meet you on the front step. Maybe she's ready to say she's sorry."

"Great," Mark said. "Then we can go play baseball." Mark grabbed his jacket and his glove. Sherman trotted after him.

Mark and Lucy met on the front step. They stared at each other.

"Sherman said you wanted to see me," Lucy said.

Mark frowned. "He told me you were ready to say you're sorry."

Sherman wagged his tail. "Come on!" he said. "Let's go for a walk. We'll go get Anne and Sergeant. Then we can all play baseball."

Lucy looked at Mark. "I guess that's better than spending the afternoon in my room."

"Yeah," Mark agreed.

"So, say you're sorry and let's go," said Sherman.

"I'm sorry I pushed you, Lucy," Mark said slowly.

"And I'm sorry I told on you," Lucy added.

"But I'm not sorry at all that I'm not going to the library," Sherman said as he wagged his tail.

"You sneak," cried Lucy.

"Come on, Lucy," said Mark. "Let's get going before you have a fight with Sherman!"

Reflecting on the story

It never feels good to be in the middle of a fight. When our friends fight, they often want us to pick a side. But then the fight gets bigger. Jesus taught his friends to be peacemakers. That means looking for ways to stop our friends from fighting and to get people talking instead of arguing.

Talking about the story

- Think of a time when you found yourself in the middle of a fight between other people. How did you feel? What did you do?
- Why do you think Jesus asked people to be peacemakers?
- Does the world needs peacemakers today? Where?

Praying after the story

Dear God,

When we find ourselves in the middle of a fight, help us be peacemakers. Give us love and courage to set things right without shouting or shoving. Even when we're mad at someone, help us find a way to say "I'm sorry" and be friends again. Amen.

Cat Attack!

Lucy came inside carrying a box.

"What's in the box?" asked Sherman.

She smiled and whispered, "A cat."

"A cat? What are you doing with a cat?" Sherman demanded. "I'm allergic to cats."

"Shhh," said Lucy. "Marsha bought this kitten for her mother's birthday. If she gives the cat to her mother as a present, her mother has to let Marsha keep it! But the party's not until Saturday, so I said I would keep the cat till then. Okay, Mom?" Lucy asked as her mother walked into the kitchen.

"I suppose so," she said. "What's the cat's name?"

"Fluffy," answered Lucy. Just then Fluffy stuck her head out of the box and smiled at everyone.

"Hmmph," said Sherman. "Fluffy? Looks like a hairball to me!"

"Come on, Sherman," said Lucy. "Be nice. If Fluffy works out, maybe I can get a kitten, too."

"What do you need a kitten for? You've got me. And I hate cats," Sherman announced. Then he marched out of the kitchen.

So Fluffy stayed in the kitchen and Sherman lay on the couch in the den.

That night the family went out shopping. As she put on her coat, Lucy said to Sherman, "Keep an eye on Fluffy while we're gone, okay?"

"That hairball?" Sherman opened one eye and looked at Lucy. "Only if you bring me a hamburger when you come back." Then he closed his eyes.

A few minutes later, Sherman felt a paw on his nose.

"Get your foot off my nose, Hairball. I hate cats," he said.

"Why do you hate cats, Bonebreath?" asked Fluffy.

"Dogs are supposed to hate cats," he announced.

"But you don't even know me. I'm fluffy and cute," said the kitten.

"I hate fluffy cats, too," Sherman said.

"Aw, come on," coaxed Fluffy. "Let's play football with this ball of yarn. It will be fun. If you beat me, you can eat me." Fluffy smiled from ear to ear.

"A cat who plays football?" Sherman asked in surprise.

"Sure. You try to wrap the yarn around the sofa. I'll try to wrap the yarn around the TV. The winner gets the hamburger." Fluffy smiled again.

"Hey, I thought cats were stupid, but you're pretty smart. Catch this pass," Sherman said and tossed the yarn in the air.

Sherman and Fluffy raced around the den with the yarn. They tied up the sofa and the TV and a chair or two. Sherman had the last bit of yarn in his mouth as he dived under the sofa. "I win, Hairball!"

Just then the car drove up. "Oh no, I'm stuck," he said, squirming. "Quick, Fluffy. Help me get out of here."

As the front door opened, Fluffy bit Sherman's tail.

"Eeow!" Sherman yelped. He jumped so hard he popped out from under the couch.

"There. I saved your life," said the kitten with a big smile.

The two of them were tangled up in a spider-web of yarn when Lucy came into the den.

Lucy shrieked, "Fluffy, you naughty cat! Look what you did with that yarn!"

She pushed Fluffy out of the room and came back with Sherman's hamburger. Lucy stroked him as she untangled him.

"Poor Sherman," said Lucy. "Did that cat bite your tail?"

After Sherman ate the burger, he said, "You know, Lucy, that cat is not so bad. We had a really good game of football."

"We? You mean you made this mess, too?" Lucy asked as she rolled up the yarn.

"Sure. But I won the game, so I got the burger," Sherman added.

"I thought you were allergic to cats," Lucy frowned.

"Not all cats, Lucy. Just hairballs," Sherman said with a big smile.

Reflecting on the story

Do you know any cats and dogs that get along? Or do they always fight "like cats and dogs"? Sometimes we think people who are different on the outside can't be our friends. But how do we know what someone is really like? Sherman found he could have fun with Fluffy once he got to know her.

God made us to be friends and neighbours together in the Church, no matter how different we seem on the outside. Let's look for friends from the inside out!

Talking about the story

- How are people different from each other? How are people the same as each other?
- Think of a friend you know. How is that friend different from you? Why do you like that friend?
- Why do you think God makes so many different people in the world?

Praying after the story

Dear God,

You made each one of us a little different from the others. Yet you made us to be friends and neighbours. Help us be good friends, even when we're as different as cats and dogs. Amen.

Fetch!

Author's note: This story is somewhat longer than average, and is designed for a worship service in which children participate throughout. It may need editing when less than ten minutes is available.

Faith theme:
We praise God in many ways. We tell the world about God's love.

Life situation:
Learning something new

Feelings:
Confidence

"Let's play Fetch," Lucy said to Sherman one day.

"Fetch? What's Fetch?" asked Sherman.

"It's a game. You'll see." Lucy picked up a stick and threw it across the yard. "Fetch, Sherman."

"What?" asked Sherman.

"Go get it," Lucy said. "Fetch the stick. Bring it here."

"Why?" asked Sherman.

"Because I said so," said Lucy. "All dogs fetch. So go fetch the stick."

"Okay, okay," said Sherman. He waddled across the yard and picked up the stick. "Now what?"

"Bring it here," called Lucy.

When Sherman dropped the stick, Lucy picked it up and threw it again. "Fetch, Sherman."

"What? Again? I just brought it back. You go get it if you want it." Sherman just sat there.

"No, no," said Lucy. "You have to fetch it. That's how this game works."

"This is a dumb game," Sherman thought as he went after the stick. He dropped it at Lucy's feet a second time. He warned her, "If you throw that again, you can fetch it yourself."

"But Sherman, you are doing very well. You're such a smart dog. You catch on so quickly." Lucy patted Sherman.

He wagged his tail. He thought he was pretty smart, too. "Thank you, Lucy."

Then Lucy picked up the stick and threw it. "Fetch, Sherman."

As Sherman ran after the stick, he thought, "Here I go again! Maybe I'm not as smart as I think I am."

When Sherman brought the stick this time, Lucy had a treat for him. "Good dog. Here's a biscuit. That's for being such a clever dog."

"Hmmm," thought Sherman as he crunched his dog biscuit, "maybe Fetch is not such a bad game after all."

Next morning Lucy said to Sherman, "Let's play Fetch!" Sherman went along, hoping for more dog biscuits. This time Lucy had a newspaper tied with string. She threw it across the grass and said, "Fetch the paper, Sherman."

Sherman ran to the newspaper, grabbed it, and gave it a good hard shake. "Grrrr!" Then he brought it back to Lucy.

"Sherman," said Lucy, "Look at the paper. You tore big holes in it. Now no one will be able to read it."

Sherman felt a little silly. "You didn't tell me you were going to read the paper, Lucy."

Lucy patted his head. "You'll be fine. You're smart. Try it again but don't shake the paper this time."

They worked all morning. Lucy threw the paper in many different places. Sherman ran to get it and dropped it at her feet. At lunchtime, Lucy hugged him and said, "Sherman, you're fantastic. I think you're ready to show off. Here are some dog biscuits."

Sherman felt quite proud as Lucy explained her plan.

The next morning after breakfast, Lucy's dad said to her, "Sweetheart, will you go fetch the paper from the front step?"

Lucy winked at Sherman and opened the back door. "Fetch the paper, Sherman."

Sherman ran out the door, around the house, grabbed the paper off the front step and brought it to Lucy. He dropped it at her feet. "Here's the paper, Dad," she said.

Everyone stared at Sherman.

"Isn't he the greatest?" Lucy asked. "He's the smartest dog in the whole world." She gave him a big hug.

Lucy's dad gave Sherman a steak bone. Mark thought Sherman should be on TV. Their Mom wondered if Sherman could fetch milk from the corner store. That night, as Sherman climbed onto Lucy's bed, she hugged him again.

"Oh, Sherman, I'm so proud of you. Thank you for fetching the paper."

"Anytime, Lucy," Sherman said, yawning happily. He felt good.

As Lucy got under the covers, she let out a shriek. "Ick. There is something cold and hard and wet in this bed." She reached under the covers and pulled out Sherman's stick.

"Want to play Fetch?" asked Sherman.

Reflecting on the story

Do you know what "praise" is? Praise is telling someone what a good job they did. Praise is telling someone how much we enjoy what they did. Praise is telling someone why we're glad to know them. What did Lucy do to praise Sherman in this story?

We come to church to praise God, to thank God for all the wonderful things in God's world, and to tell the world how glad we are that we belong to God.

Talking about the story

- Remember a time when someone praised you for something you did.
- How do you feel when someone tells you that you did something well?
- What are some good things that God has done for us in the world?
- How do we praise God for those good things?

Praying after the story

Dear God,

We praise you for your love. You love us so much that you are always with us. We praise you for all the beautiful things you have made in this world. Help us praise you day by day. We will show our love for you by caring for each other in Jesus' name. Amen.

Presenting Jackie Rabbit

Jackie Rabbit Makes a Choice

Author's note: This story is the first story in the Jackie Rabbit series. It can be used to introduce other stories in the series.

Marvin the Magician walked onto the stage, which was just an old red circus wagon. He called out to the children crowded around him. "Have you seen my beautiful assistant, Jacqueline, anywhere?"

"No!" cried a little boy in the front row. "She's not here."

"What does she look like, Mister?" asked the little boy's sister.

Jackie sat in the dark, waiting. "Why doesn't Marvin get a new act?" she wondered. "It's the same old line every time."

Marvin went on, "Oh no! She must be here. She's never late. The show cannot go on without Jacqueline." He paused.

"Oh! Oh! Ohhh!" squealed Marvin. "I think… I think I have found her. Why yes, here she is. Ladies and gentlemen, girls and boys, my lovely assistant, Jacqueline."

With a magical wave, Marvin pulled Jackie out of his sleeve by her ears. He kept her dangling before the laughing children.

"Voila, my friends. Here she is! Jackie Rabbit!" Marvin cried.

"Marvin!" Jackie whispered. "Put me down before my ears come off."

Faith theme:
God guides us.

Life situation:
Making a very important choice

Feelings:
Worry about the future

How Jackie Rabbit hated her job. Marvin plunked her down on the table in front of him. Then he made a pigeon appear and set it on her head.

"Ugh!" thought Jackie. "Cold feet again." She said to herself, "I've had it. I'm getting out of show business! Let's see how Marvin likes *my* disappearing act."

While Marvin searched for magic coins and made them appear behind children's ears, Jackie Rabbit made a flying leap off the stage. The pigeon squawked and flapped its wings. Jackie hopped through the crowd of little feet and headed for the parking lot.

"Jacqueline, come back!" called Marvin. "I'll give you extra carrots – twice a week."

But there was no stopping Jackie Rabbit. She was at the roadside before she paused to catch her breath.

"Which way shall I go?" she wondered.

Across the road she could see a meadow with a forest beyond it. Down the road Jackie knew she would find the town where the circus had been the day before. Up the road, who could say? Jackie Rabbit could hear Marvin's feet thumping as he ran after her.

Jackie took a deep breath. Then she dashed away to start a new life – without the circus.

Can you guess which way she went? Jackie Rabbit went to town. She was a circus rabbit who knew more about circus wagons and candy floss than meadows and grass. With no one to help her, Jackie Rabbit had to follow her nose and use her wits to make a new life for herself.

Reflecting on the story

As we grow up, we have lots of choices to make. What kind of person do you want to be? Where would you like to live? What would you like to do? Sometimes it's hard to know what to do or where to start. If you ever wonder what to do or which way to turn, remember you are not alone. God will help you make wise choices.

Talking about the story

- If you were Jackie Rabbit, which way would you have gone?
- What kind of work would you like to do when you grow up?
- What important choices do you have to make? Make a list and then say a prayer asking God to help you choose well.

Praying after the story

Dear God,

Whenever I have a choice to make, help me figure out what to do. Guide me to make wise choices so that I can follow Jesus as I grow up. Amen.

Jackie Rabbit Goes to Town

Jackie Rabbit used to be a circus rabbit. She could pop out of hats and slide out of sleeves. But Jackie was unhappy in the circus, popping and sliding. So one day she ran away from the circus to start a new life.

Jackie Rabbit knew that if she wanted enough carrots to eat in her new life, she would have to get a job.

"What can I do?" she wondered. She had been a circus rabbit all her life. "I've been in a magic show every day I can remember. All I can do is pop out of hats and balance pigeons on my head."

The first place she stopped was a grocery store run by a porcupine named Mr. Stickler.

"Do you need some help in your store?" Jackie asked. "I need a job and I know all about vegetables. Especially lettuce and carrots."

Mr. Stickler nodded. "I could use someone to help me take money at the front counter. Can you count?" he asked.

Jackie said, "Sure. Up to three. One, two, three. Everything in magic shows happens on the count of three."

"Sorry," said Mr. Stickler. "But three isn't high enough. In this store, we have to count up to 10 or 20 or even 50!"

Jackie hopped away sadly. "Maybe I could work in an office," she thought, "with a computer and floppy disks. Rabbits are very good with floppy things."

But when Jackie asked for a job at an office, she found that they needed someone who could spell and speak French.

"The only French word I know is Abracadabra," Jackie sighed.

Then Jackie went to the library. "I'm Jackie Rabbit," she said to the children's librarian. "I like children and I'm very quiet. A library would be the perfect place for me to work."

"Can you read aloud?" the librarian whispered.

"No," whispered Jackie. "Rabbits can't do anything loud. I can't read either. No one has to read in the circus."

"Tsk, tsk," tsked the librarian. "Then how could you work in a library?"

Jackie sighed and hopped towards the door. "I can't read and I can't spell and I can only count to three. What will I ever do?" she wondered. "Will I have to go back to the circus?"

"You could be my baby bunny sitter," said a gentle voice behind her.

Jackie turned around. There stood a rabbit with a big armload of library books and at least ten baby bunnies hopping in circles around her.

"I'm Harriet Hopper," she said. "And these are my little Hoppers. If you worked in a circus, you'll feel right at home in our hutch. By the time you get to know my babies, you'll be able to count to ten – or fifteen next month. More baby bunnies on the way!" Harriet smiled. "Will you come home with us, Jackie Rabbit?"

Jackie nodded. She smiled at the two biggest bunnies. "I can teach you to balance a pigeon on your head," she said.

"All right!" cheered the little bunnies.

Jackie Rabbit had just found her first job.

Reflecting on the story

There is so much to learn in God's world. Some days it seems we will never know everything we need to know! No matter how old we are, or how much we know already, there is always something new to learn. But no matter how old we are, or how much we still have to learn, there are things we can do to help each other and care for God's world today.

Talking about the story

- What do you want to learn to do? How will you learn it?
- What can you already do to help God care for this world?

Praying after the story

Dear God,

As I grow, teach me what I need to know. Help me learn new things day by day, and show me what I can do today to help you care for this world. Amen.

A Bunch of Bunnies

Author's note: This story is somewhat longer than average. It may need editing for a worship setting.

Jackie Rabbit had a new job. She was the baby bunny sitter for Harriet Hopper's ten little bunnies. Jackie had never seen so many baby bunnies! There were two tiny ones, two little ones, two a bit bigger and four who were all the same size, the biggest of all.

Harriet said, "These little Hoppers will keep you on your toes. They can get into mischief before you can say...." Just then, the four biggest bunnies picked up a little bunny and began to stuff it into a hole in a tree.

"Abracadabra!" said Jackie with a grin. They watched as another bunny disappeared down the hole.

"Come and meet them. It will take you a day to learn their names!" said Harriet.

Jackie met Hoppy and Floppy, the tiny ones who were stuck in the hole. Jumper and Thumper were waiting for their turn. The four biggest bunnies, Puff, Muff, Fluff and Spotty, were hopping up and down.

"A new baby bunny sitter! Hooray! Can you catch us, Jackie? Can you tell us apart?"

Jackie smiled and said, "Not yet, Puff."

"I'm Muff," said the bunny. "She's Puff. See how her tail puffs?"

Harriet rolled her eyes. "You'll learn, Jackie. Now where are Bucky and Lucky? Are they down

Faith theme:
We are part of God's family. We help each other.

Life situation:
Learning something new

Feelings:
Worrying about doing the wrong thing

that hole, too? Keep them busy, Jackie, while I make lunch."

Jackie gathered the bunnies around the tree. "I'll tell you stories about the circus," she said. The bunnies were all ears. "One day the clown was walking on stilts. His stilts were so tall that he walked up to the trapeze to have a swing. But then he was afraid to jump down, so we had to call the fire truck to rescue him." The bunnies giggled.

Jackie told the bunnies about the lion tamer who was allergic to cats and kept sneezing in the lion's mouth. And about her days popping out of hats and sliding out of sleeves. By lunchtime the bunnies were tired out from laughing. After lunch, Harriet and Jackie put the bunnies to bed in a big hammock stretched between two trees. As they rocked the hammock, the bunnies fell asleep.

Jackie sighed. "I don't know how you do it! These bunnies are an awful pawful."

The next day Harriet said, "Jackie, it's your turn. Give the bunnies lunch while I go shopping. I haven't been shopping without bunnies underfoot for months."

Jackie gulped. "Do you think I can do it?" Harriet just smiled.

Jackie looked at lunch lined up on the table. There was carrot goo for Hoppy and Floppy; carrot stew for Jumper and Thumper; carrot soup for Bucky and Lucky; and new carrots to chew for Puff, Muff, Fluff and Spotty. "Come on, bunnies! Lunchtime," called Jackie.

Hoppy and Floppy slurped the carrot goo, but before long, they were rubbing the goo on each other. "You look funny turning orange," giggled Floppy.

"Stop that, you two!" said Jackie. Then Jumper and Thumper wouldn't eat carrot stew.

"We want the soup! We want the soup!" they cried.

"It's stew for you," said Bucky.

"The soup is for us," said Lucky.

As Jackie sorted out the bowls, she saw a carrot fly by. The four big bunnies weren't chewing! They threw their new carrots all over the place. They even stuck them in their ears.

"Oh my," said Jackie Rabbit.

"Give us carrot cake! We want carrot cake. Carrot cake for lunch!" The four biggest bunnies began to cheer and soon all ten bunnies wanted carrot cake.

So Jackie Rabbit sliced up carrot cake. "If I give you cake, will you take a nap?"

The little bunnies jumped into the hammock after lunch. "Swing us, Jackie! Higher! Higher!"

As Jackie rocked the hammock, she told the story about the clown swinging back and forth, back and forth, on the trapeze. Then she sang "Rock-a-bye Bunny on the treetop" with ten verses, one for each bunny. When she had finished, the little bunnies were fast asleep.

Jackie went back to the kitchen. What a mess! There was goo on the floor and a bowl of soup turned upside down. New carrots lay everywhere. Jackie shook her head.

Just then Harriet Hopper walked in. Jackie gulped.

"Oh no!" she cried. "Please don't look at this mess! Give me time to clean it up!"

Harriet just smiled. "Jackie, lunchtime is always like this. I'll help you scrape up that goo."

"You mean you're not angry with me?" Jackie was surprised.

Harriet laughed. "Ten little bunnies make more mess than a circus in town! Every day!" She handed Jackie a broom and picked up a rag. "Good thing you were in a magic show, Jackie. You can help me make this mess disappear!"

Reflecting on the story

A big family means lots of things to do. When we belong to a big family, we work together to get things done. The Church is God's big family. There are many things to do to care for each other and to touch the world with God's love. When we work together, the job doesn't seem quite so big.

Talking about the story

- What are some things you do to help out in your family?
- What are some things you see people do to help out in the Church?
- What are some things you can do as part of God's family?

Praying after the story

Dear God,

I am glad to be part of your big family. I'm glad you love the world, even when the world is in a mess. Show us what we can do together to touch the world with your love. Amen.

Finders Keepers?

Jackie Rabbit was looking for a new job. She had run out of carrots and she was very hungry. She was hopping sadly down the street when she tripped over something.

It was a small brown paper bag.

Jackie picked up the bag and peeked inside. She couldn't believe her eyes.

"Carrots! Three big, juicy carrots! It's a gift from my fairy godrabbit," Jackie thought.

She was so hungry she pulled out the biggest carrot and ate it right away. "Finders keepers, losers weepers," she thought. "I really needed that carrot."

As Jackie Rabbit pulled out a second carrot to eat, she noticed that there was something else in the bag.

It was a small purse.

"Uh-oh," thought Jackie. "I don't think fairy godrabbits carry purses."

Jackie opened the purse. Inside she found some money and some papers and a card. On the card it said 'Edna P. Bunny – 56 Cabbage Lane.'

"What shall I do?" Jackie wondered. "I'm so hungry, I want to eat all these carrots right now. I guess I could eat the carrots and take the purse back. Or maybe I could take a dollar and buy some more carrots and then take the purse back. Or I could just keep everything. After all, finders keepers, losers weepers."

Jackie sighed a long sigh as she thought about what to do.

Faith theme:
Jesus asks us to treat others the way we like to be treated.

Life situation:
Finding something someone else lost

Feelings:
Temptation, relief

219

Then Jackie stood up straight. "What if Edna P. Bunny is like the old rabbit who lived in a shoe who had so many bunnies she didn't know what to do? What if Edna P. Bunny needs these carrots to feed her little bunnies?"

Jackie felt sorry that she had eaten even one carrot. "I'm going to take everything back to Edna P. Bunny."

Jackie Rabbit hopped through town until she found 56 Cabbage Lane. She knocked softly on the door and held her breath. A little old rabbit with glasses perched halfway down her nose opened the door.

"Are you Edna P. Bunny?" Jackie asked.

"Why, yes, I am," said the old rabbit. "How can I help you, dear?"

Jackie swallowed and said, "I think I can help you. Did you lose this purse?"

"Jumping jackrabbits!" said Edna. "So there it is! I've been hunting for that purse for two days. Thanks for finding it. My only pictures of my new grandbunnies are inside that purse." Edna was so happy she hopped up and down.

Jackie Rabbit bit her lip. "I have to tell you something, Edna P. Bunny. The purse was in this bag with three carrots. I was so hungry I ate one before I noticed your purse. I'm...uh...very sorry that I ate your carrot."

Edna P. Bunny smiled. "That's quite all right, dear. There are lots more carrots in my garden. Please come in. Let's have tea. And I'll show you all the pictures of all my grandbunnies."

Jackie Rabbit spent the afternoon with Edna P. Bunny, eating carrot cake and cabbage cookies and drinking parsnip tea. Together they looked at about a hundred pictures of little bunnies who mostly looked alike to Jackie Rabbit.

At the door, Edna P. Bunny said, "Thank you, dear, for having tea with an old bunny. I want you to take this money for being such a fine rabbit and finding my pictures. Please come back and have tea another time."

Jackie Rabbit blushed and said thank you. When she looked in her paw, she saw that Edna P. Bunny had given her five dollars. "I didn't find a purse today," she thought. "I found a good friend."

Reflecting on the story

Did you ever hear the saying "Finders keepers, losers weepers"? It means that we want to keep whatever we find. But when we say that, we forget that what we have found might be very important to the person who lost it.

Jesus had a saying, too: "In everything, do to others as you would have them do to you" (Matthew 7.12). When we lose something important, we're glad if someone finds it and brings it back to us. So that's what we should do if we find something that belongs to someone else! And maybe we'll find a friend, too.

Talking about the story

- Have you ever lost something important? How did you feel? Did you get it back?
- Have you ever found something important? How did you feel? What did you do?

Praying after the story

Dear God,

When I find something, I often feel like keeping it. When I lose something, I am so glad to get it back. Help me look for the person who lost whatever we find. Help us help each other, whenever we can, just as Jesus taught us. Amen.

Outfoxed!

Faith theme:
God guides us.

Life situation:
Wondering who can be trusted

Feelings:
Stubbornness

"Sam! Sam! Guess what? I got a new job!" Jackie Rabbit hopped up and down in great excitement. Her friend Sam Squirrel was sitting on a park bench, feeding pigeons.

"What's the job this time, Jackie?" Sam asked.

"I'm going to be an actress!" said Jackie. "I tried out for the leading role in *Peter Rabbit*. Sly Fox Productions is making a new movie and I'm going to be the star!"

"Sly Fox Productions?" frowned Sam. "You're not mixed up with Sly, that crafty old fox? He's always up to no good!"

"Don't call my friend Sly bad names," Jackie said with her nose in the air. "He's going to make me a star. First, *Peter Rabbit*. Then he'll take me to Hollywood and introduce me to Walt Disney and all the famous rabbits in the world. He promised."

Sam shook his head. "I bet Sly Fox will invite you down to his den and eat you for supper, Jackie!"

Jackie Rabbit got very angry. "Stop it! Don't say mean things about Sly Fox. You're just jealous because I'm going to be a star. I don't want to be your friend anymore. You're mean as a badger and twice as ugly." Jackie started to hop away. Then she turned back and said to Sam, "I *am* going to Sly's den for supper tonight to talk about *our* movie. I hope your toes fall off. So there!"

Jackie Rabbit hopped off in a rage. Sam sighed. "I hope she'll be all right," he said, shaking his head.

The next day, Sam was walking through the park. On the bench where he had been sitting the day before he noticed a rabbit. The rabbit had a paper bag pulled over its head. The paper bag was sniffling.

"Jackie?" Sam asked. "Is that you, the famous movie rabbit, inside that paper bag?"

The paper bag nodded.

"What's wrong?" asked Sam. "Why are you crying?"

"Because," the bag sniffled, "you were right and I was wrong. And now you won't be my friend anymore." SNIFFFF!

Sam pulled the bag off Jackie's head. "Jackie, I'm still your friend. Tell me what happened."

Jackie Rabbit poured out her story. There was no movie. There was no trip to Hollywood. Sly would get her a job as an Easter Bunny in a big store if she promised to be his house rabbit all winter. If she wouldn't work for him, Sly Fox was going to eat her for dinner.

"I said all those mean things to you, Sam," Jackie sobbed, "when you were my best friend after all. Will you ever forgive me?" SNIFFFF!

"Sure!" said Sam with a smile.

"You will?" Jackie was surprised.

"What else are friends for?" said Sam.

"I hope your toes didn't fall off," added Jackie.

"All present and accounted for," smiled Sam. "Come on! Let's get some breakfast and you can tell me how you got away from Sly Fox."

"Oh," said Jackie. "That was easy. I pretended to clean his house. Then I sucked his tail into the vacuum cleaner! I guess that means I'm not cut out to be a house rabbit."

"I guess not," agreed Sam, flicking his tail in the air.

Reflecting on the story

As we grow up, we have to learn when to say 'yes' and when to say 'no.' We have to learn what is safe and what is dangerous. We have to learn who makes a good friend and who cannot be trusted. There's no easy way to tell. But we can learn to make wise choices when we talk with the people who love us and keep us safe. We can ask God to guide us when we have an important choice to make.

Talking about the story

- What kind of person makes a good friend?
- How do you decide whether you should trust somebody?
- If you weren't sure whether you should trust somebody, who are some wise people you could ask for help?

Praying after the story
Dear God,

Thank you for the wise and loving people in my life. Whenever I have an important choice to make, show me whom I can trust and how to be safe. Help me grow up to be wise and loving, too. Amen.

The Advent Adventures of Jackie Rabbit

Author's note: This story, which is in three parts, is designed to be told over three Sundays in Advent.

Introduction
Jackie Rabbit was once a famous circus rabbit who had popped out of hats and slid out of sleeves for most of her life. Then one day she ran away from the circus. Since then, she has had a lot of jobs as she tries to make her way in the world.

She has a friend named Sam who is a red squirrel with a good attitude. For someone who plays in the park a lot, Sam knows a lot about life. Just like you do. Sometimes Jackie finds herself in the middle of a muddle, even when Sam gives her good advice. Today we're going to hear the first part of one of Jackie's adventures.

Part 1 – Jackie Gets a Message

"Sam! Sam!" Jackie Rabbit came bouncing up to Sam on the sidewalk one morning. "I did it! I got a job!"

Sam the Squirrel smiled and shook his head. "Jackie Rabbit, you are always getting jobs. Is this one for keeps?"

"For sure," said Jackie. "I am now a delivery rabbit for the Flying Hare Express."

"What are you going to deliver? Newspapers? Groceries? I sure hope it's newspapers. You'd break eggs the way you hop!" Sam took a big hop himself and landed hard on the sidewalk. "Oooof! There go the eggs."

Jackie sniffed. "I deliver important messages and packages to animals in the forest. I already have my first assignment." She waved an envelope under Sam's nose. "It's a letter for Bertie the Badger."

Sam snorted. "You? In the forest? You've never been in the forest before, Jackie. You're a city rabbit. You'll get lost. You'll freeze in the snow."

"Hmmph!" said Jackie. "I won't get lost – I have a map. I won't freeze – I have a scarf and my own fur coat."

Sam smiled and flicked his tail. "Why don't you wait until tomorrow? I'll come with you if we can leave in the morning."

Jackie shook her head. "This message can't wait. I promised to deliver it as soon as I can. A delivery rabbit always keeps her promise."

Sam waved goodbye as Jackie Rabbit set off with her message, her map, and a carrot for supper.

When she reached the edge of town, Jackie stopped to check her map.

"Climb the old stone fence and cross the grassy meadow. That's easy," she said as she hopped over the crunchy snow. But by the time she reached the big pine grove across the next field, it was almost too dark to read the map.

"Maybe I should sleep here tonight and get an early start in the morning," Jackie thought. "I have to keep my promise and deliver this message tomorrow."

As Jackie munched her carrot, she shivered. "It's colder in the forest than I thought. Maybe I'll build a little fire to keep warm."

But Jackie Rabbit had never built a fire before. She made a pile of twigs and sticks, and lit them with a match, but she couldn't keep them burning.

"Paper," she thought. "I need paper to light the fire."

Jackie looked at the two pieces of paper she carried – the letter she had to deliver and her map. As her toes got colder and colder, Jackie studied the map in the fading daylight.

"I can remember the way. I'm sure I can remember."

Once it was too dark to read, she scrunched up the map and stuck it into the pile of twigs. She struck a match and POOF! The fire started.

Beside that little fire, Jackie Rabbit warmed herself until she fell asleep.

In the morning, she wasn't so glad she had burned her map.

"Now which way will I go?" she asked herself. "I have to keep my promise. But I can't remember whether I go over the hill and along the stream – or over the stream and around the hill."

Which way should Jackie Rabbit go? Will she find her way? Will she be able to keep her promise? We'll have to wait for our next story to find out what happens!

Dear God,
Whenever I am not sure which way to go, come and be with me. Help me figure out what to do. Show me the right path to take, for Jesus' sake. Amen.

Part 2 – Jackie Finds Trouble

Faith theme:
God is with us. God guides us.

Life situation:
Facing a scary, even dangerous situation

Feelings:
Worry, fear

It started to snow. Jackie Rabbit pulled her scarf a bit tighter. "I think there's a path up the hill by a dead elm tree."

Jackie scooted through the snowflakes. Sure enough, there was a path!

"Now which way?" she wondered. Jackie decided to follow the path by the stream. "I won't get too lost if I stay near the stream."

Before long, the stream ended in a swamp, which was already frozen over. Jackie tiptoed carefully across the ice. The snowflakes danced and swirled around her. She hopped through a grove of maple trees and into a little meadow.

"Helloooo!" she called.

Not even a whisper answered.

Jackie sighed. "Where are the meadow mice when you need them? If I can't find someone to show me the way, I'll have to go back. But then I'd break my promise. And then I'd lose my job."

Jackie knew she couldn't go back anyway. The snow was falling so fast it had already covered her tracks across the meadow. Just then, Jackie heard a sound in the brush. "Maybe this is the place where Bertie the Badger lives!" she told herself.

"Excuse me," Jackie called politely, as she scampered around a bush. "Are you Bertie the Badger? I have a message for you."

Then she stopped. It wasn't Bertie the Badger. There was a big grey dog pawing in the snow. It turned at the sound of Jackie's voice. Its golden eyes flashed at her.

"Oh, no!" gulped Jackie. "It's a wolf!"

As the wolf smiled at her, she looked all around her. "What will I do now?" she cried. She took a big breath and dived into a snowbank.

Under the soft snow, Jackie wiggled and wiggled, burrowing deeper and deeper.

"Oh dear! A snowbank won't save me from a hungry wolf," she thought. Jackie squirmed along the ground. Suddenly she felt herself sliding down, down, down into darkness.

"A rabbit hole!" she thought. "I'm safe!" Jackie sniffed her way along the black tunnel. "I hope whoever owns this hole is on a winter vacation. Anybody home?" she whispered.

No one answered.

Safe in the hole, Jackie had time to think. "I have to deliver this letter today. If only I could get away from the wolf."

She thought a little more. "I wonder if this rabbit hole has a back door."

Jackie wiggled her way through the darkness until she could see a faint light in the distance. "An escape!" she thought. "I'll fool that old wolf."

She made her way to the next hole and took a deep breath. Jackie pushed herself through the powdery snow into the fresh air. All of a sudden she stopped. Her hind leg felt as if it was on fire. She was pulled back to earth and landed hard on the ground. With tears in her eyes, Jackie sniffed at her leg stretched out behind her.

"A snare," she groaned. "I'm trapped."

Sure enough, a loop of wire gripped her back leg. Jackie struggled. She pulled. She even nibbled at the wire. But it was no use. Her leg hurt more than ever.

Poor little Jackie Rabbit. How could anyone have so much trouble? How will she get free? We'll find out in the next adventure of Jackie Rabbit!

Dear God,

When things go wrong, I need you with me. When I'm afraid, I need you nearby. When trouble won't let go, come and help me. Show me the way through anything that goes wrong, for Jesus' sake. Amen.

Part 3 – Jackie Keeps Her Promise

The more Jackie tugged and struggled with the snare, the more her leg hurt. Tired and scared, she lay shivering in the snow, the message scrunched up in her paw. Tears slid over her nose and froze on its tip. She was so tired and so cold.

"It's no use. I can't budge. Sam was right. I'll probably freeze in the forest." Jackie closed her eyes and lay very, very still.

"Don't be afraid, little rabbit," said a voice close by.

Jackie blinked. A child was kneeling in the snow beside her.

"I'll help you," said the child.

Jackie watched as the child's fingers worked away at the wire. She couldn't tell if it was a girl or a boy. The child's hat was pulled right down to the eyes. A scarf was wrapped around and around the child's nose and chin so only the eyes peeked out.

"Friendly eyes," thought Jackie as the child continued to work.

Within a few minutes, the child freed Jackie's foot from the snare and rubbed that foot very gently with soft woollen mittens. "There!" said the child softly. "See if you can hop."

Jackie jumped a few times, carefully.

"It hurts a little," said Jackie, "but I think my leg will be all right. You saved my life," Jackie added as she turned to face the child. Then Jackie told the child all about her adventure, burning the map, losing her way, hiding from the wolf.

Faith theme:
Jesus shows us God's love. Jesus came in a surprising way!

Life situation:
Help comes In surprising ways

Feelings:
Fear, relief

"Oh, that wolf won't hurt you," the child promised. "He's my friend. I won't let him eat rabbits! If you still want to find Bertie the Badger today, look over there. His hole is just over the next hill, behind the big rock in a small clearing." The child pointed the way. "There's an easy way home, too. Down the hill and along the stream."

"Now I will be able to keep my promise!" Jackie smiled.

She turned around to say thank you, but there was nobody there.

"Hey! Where are you?" Jackie called. "I want to thank you for saving me. I don't even know your name."

Not so much as a whisper answered.

As Jackie looked around, she couldn't see any footprints in the snow. The mysterious child had disappeared.

"Thank you, whoever you are," Jackie whispered. "I'll never forget you," she added as she remembered those smiling eyes.

Then she hopped up the hill to deliver her message and keep her promise.

Reflecting after the story

At Christmastime, we remember another mysterious child – Jesus – who came to help us and to set us free. We remember that Jesus came to bring God's love to us whenever things go wrong. When we take the wrong path and lose our way, Jesus can help us find our way home. This is God's promise!

Praying after the story

Dear God,

Thank you for sending Jesus into our world to touch us with your love. Whenever I get into trouble, when I lose my way, when I'm not sure what to do, come and find me. Help me remember the love of Jesus so I can follow the path he took. Amen.

Part III

Indexes to The Story Collection
&
Sources and Resources for Follow-up

Index of Faith Themes

The index of faith themes is presented in four major sections:

- **God, Our Maker:** stories that touch on God's relationship to us and to the world
- **Jesus, Our Friend:** stories that relate to what Jesus teaches us about God's love and about our love for each other
- **God, Our Helper:** stories that show our need for God
- **In God's Family:** how we live as God's people at home, at church and with our neighbours

For each category, there are simple affirmations about God and how we understand ourselves as God's people. Stories often portray more than one of these affirmations, and so titles appear more than once.

God, Our Maker

Jesus, Our Friend

God, Our Helper

In God's Family

Index of Life Situations

There are five sections to the *Index of Life Situations:*

- Being Part of a Family
- Getting Along with Friends and Neighbours
- Making Choices
- Getting into Trouble (this section has two parts: one for trouble characters provoke by their own actions, and one for trouble that arises unprovoked)
- Exploring the World Around Us

The situation in each story has been summarized in a single phrase. The plots of some stories suggest more than a single theme; these stories appear more than once.

Being Part of a Family

Getting Along with Friends and Neighbours

Making Choices

Getting into Trouble

• Making trouble for ourselves

- **When trouble finds us**

Exploring the World Around Us

Index of Feelings
Explored in a Story

The index of feelings uses terms familiar to adults rather than language children will always recognize. Each category names the experience of the central character in the story through an emotion or a concept that interprets an emotion. Some stories provoke a range of feelings and so titles appear more than once.

Many categories suggest a problematic feeling because the model of conversation and prayer that follows the stories seeks to support children in working through challenging feelings and situations. Where a story moves through a problematic feeling to a resolution, the title is listed under both the initial and the emerging feelings.

Index of Biblical References

Throughout the first part of this book, I have made reference to Bible stories and Scripture texts that are formative for my understanding of *The Story Project*. Below is an index of these references if you wish to consult them more fully. Familiar references to stories or texts appear in regular type; short quotations from the Scripture texts appear in italics.

The Old Testament

The New Testament

Romans 8.38-39	76	*[Nothing] will be able to separate us from the love of God in Christ Jesus our Lord.*
1 Corinthians 12 Romans 12	120	A variety of gifts and members in the Body of Christ
2 Corinthians 13.13	95	*The grace of the Lord Jesus Christ, the love of God, and the communion of the Holy Spirit be with all of you.*
Galatians 3.26-28	120	*All of you are one in Christ Jesus.*
Revelation 4	70	The vision of the Heavenly Throne room: *Holy, holy, holy*
Revelation 7.17	99	*God will wipe away every tear from their eyes.*
Revelation 21, 22	75	The vision of the holy City, the New Jerusalem

Sources and Resources for Follow-up

Understanding Children as People of Faith

In Christian tradition over the centuries, children's capacity to relate to God has been interpreted in various ways. Psychologists of our own time also differ in the ways they name and evaluate children's developing abilities. *The Story Project* did not set out to test or take a stand on such differences, although my perspective is named in Part I of this book. Here are some resources that have helped me understand children and think carefully about how to interact with them as people of faith. These resources do not share one perspective, but they focus on the importance of our relationships with children as people of faith whom God loves and encounters.

Anderson, Herbert & Johnson, Susan

Regarding Children: A New Respect for Childhood and Families. Louisville, KY: Westminster/ John Knox Press, 1994.

This book is mentioned in Chapter 4. Anderson presents an encouraging view of the importance of family life for children as they grow. He combines his research as a pastoral theologian with stories and examples provided by Susan Johnson, a parish pastor, as well as by many parents. The book challenges congregations to consider their role in children's lives.

Berends, Polly B.   *Gently Lead: How to Teach Your Children About God While Finding out for Yourself.* New York: Harper Collins, 1991.

This very readable collection covers a wide range of spiritual themes, with introductory comments on each from the author, who is a counsellor and children's author. She provides examples of conversations with children and some wonderful poetry to appeal to a child's ear. She intends the book for people both "in" and "out" of organized denominations.

Bunge, Marcia, ed.   *The Child in Christian Thought.* Grand Rapids, MI: W.B. Eerdmans, 2001.

This collection of essays is for those who want to sample the history of Christian thinking on children. Authors come from a wide variety of Christian traditions and examine both ancient and contemporary views on the place of children in Christian community.

Coles, Robert   *The Moral Intelligence of Children.* New York: Random House, 1997. *The Spiritual Life of Children.* Boston: Houghton Mifflin, 1991.

Coles' work with children from around the world is introduced in Chapter 1. These are but two of his many books that report on his interviews with children on a number of subjects.

The Moral Intelligence of Children will be very helpful to parents and teachers who are concerned about understanding the way children draw on values in making moral decisions as they grow. *The Spiritual Life of Children* illustrates how children talk about God and their concerns for the world, drawing on comments from participants in a variety of religious traditions and from those with no religious affiliation.

Fowler, James   *Stages of Faith: The Psychology of Human Development and the Quest for Meaning.* New York: Harper Collins, 1981, 1995.

This pioneer work examines how children develop and express faith as they grow. Fowler draws on the theories of Jean Piaget in education and Lawrence Kohlberg in moral development. His model has been criticized for over-emphasizing the cognitive aspects of children's growing abilities. Nevertheless, in listening to children quite close in age and recognizing unique and subtle features in the ways they talk about faith, I have found his examples helpful. His interviews span the life cycle and also provoke self-examination in adults about our own faith journeys.

Halverson, Delia   *How Do Our Children Grow? Introducing Children to God, Jesus, the Bible, Prayer, Church.* Nashville, TN: Abingdon Press, 1993.

As her title suggests, Halverson considers important themes in Christian faith chapter by chapter. She moves back and forth between analysis and storytelling and offers many useful suggestions for exploring these large topics with young children.

Myers, B. & Wm.   *Engaging Transcendence: The Church's Ministry & Covenant with Young Children.* Cleveland, OH: The Pilgrim Press, 1992.

This work expands analysis and advocacy based on children's profound sense of transcendence and wonder. It offers some thought-provoking ideas for both parents and church leaders to consider, arguing for effective participation of children in the life of the Church. There are helpful insights from religious educators and important examples taken from children's literature and children's lives.

Robinson, Edward   *Original Vision: A Study of the Religious Experience of Childhood.* New York: The Seabury Press, 1983.

Robinson offers a fascinating range of stories drawn from his correspondence with adults remembering religious ideas and experiences from their childhoods. The book identifies common themes from this research, supporting Robinson's appreciation for the depth and significance of children's religious experience. He offers a valuable critique of Jean Piaget and Sigmund Freud and their influence on common assumptions about children's capacities.

Westerhoff, John H. III   *Bringing up Children in the Christian Faith.* Minneapolis: Winston Press, 1980.

This classic essay encourages parents to understand their relationships with their children as God-given opportunities to grow in faith together. Westerhoff emphasizes the integrity of a child's faith as the child grows. He offers sample responses to common questions about God and encourages families to pray together. He concludes with a model for spiritual life that can engage both adult and child in relationship with God.

Working with Children as People of Faith

Here are some examples of material that can be used with children to enrich their prayer and worship participation. There are a few sources for answering questions, too! I notice that most children's bookstores stock a wide collection of prayer books and books with information on religious traditions suitable for different age groups. It is impossible to suggest the most helpful titles in an ever-changing list, so be sure to look in your local bookstore and library. Ask for help if you need some guidance about choosing resources for a child of a particular age.

Chesto, Kathleen *Family Prayer for Family Times: Traditions, Celebrations and Rituals.* Mystic, CT: Twenty-Third Publications, 1995.

This book is full of creative ideas for families seeking to integrate spiritual life into family occasions. Its resources include Prayer throughout the Day, Rituals for Family Time and Rituals for Special Times of the Year. Language in the prayers is appropriate for quite young children. The author, a Roman Catholic, reflects her tradition in some of the liturgies. Most of her creative ideas will appeal to families of any Christian denomination.

Eibner, Janet M. &
Walker, Susan G.

God, Kids, & Us: The Growing Edge of Ministry with Children and The People Who Care for Them. Toronto: United Church Publishing House/Anglican Book Centre, 1996.

This work has very practical ideas both for congregational programs for children and for families committed to the active participation of children in the life of the Church. The authors provide helpful advice and instruction for adults preparing to work with children. There are also recipes, prayers, stories with questions and even sample worksheets to prepare for group activities.

Holm, Marilyn F.

Tell Me Why: A Guide to Children's Questions about Faith & Life. Minneapolis: Augsburg Press, 1985.

This book comes recommended by a minister and children's leaders in a small congregation. It covers a huge range of questions from children on theological themes and family situations. It provides a good framework on concerns that lurk behind questions. It tends to explain topics and may sometimes reach too far for quite young children. Its combination of faith questions and life issues such as death and remarriage is very helpful.

McCaslin, Susan

Thinking about God. Mystic, CT: Twenty-Third Publications, 1994.

Here is a book to read to a young child with questions about God our Maker. It is posed as a conversation between a mother and a child. There are some delightful images that will appeal to a child's tangible experience of the world and its creatures. The child gives voice to her own opinions and her mother explores those ideas with her in an appreciative way.

Marrocco, Nancy   *Homemade Christians: A Guide for Parents of Young Children.* Ottawa: Novalis, 1985.

I was introduced to this book as a gift suggestion for parents when a baby is baptized. It offers encouragement in the role for parents to introduce very young children to God and to the Church community. There are some very practical suggestions to use with young children as well as themes for parents to talk about together.

Payden, D.A. &   *Celebrating at Home: Prayers and Liturgies*
Loving, Laura   *for Families.* Cleveland: United Church Press, 1998.

This collection of resources for families to use at home is especially helpful for those whose churches follow the Christian Year in worship. There is a short teaching section introducing seasons and celebrations in the Christian Year, followed by ideas for liturgies and prayers. The language is suitable for older children and adults, for the most part.

Stewart, Sonja &   *Young Children and Worship.* Louisville,
Berryman, Jerome   KY: Westminster/John Knox Press, 1989.

This book is mentioned in Chapter 4 as a resource to help children develop reverence for holy space and time. It is also a fascinating and well-respected introduction to a set of resources used by churches of many denominations to introduce young children to the shape of Christian worship through patterns of participation appropriate for those as young as age three. The authors offer very helpful suggestions on ways to speak with young children to open up their sense of wonder about God and the world.

Facing Sorrow and Difficulty as People of Faith

This group of resources has material primarily for adults, though a couple of books look at children's issues when facing grief or loss. This theme often raises the most difficult spiritual issues for believers, whatever our age. Sometimes reading a book offers a new perspective on events that have been very painful for us, or perhaps introduces a new way of thinking about God. Christian tradition and its roots in Hebrew Scripture offer many ways to speak of God's concern for us in times of suffering. These books do not offer the same perspective, but speak with many different voices from the deep faith of people who have suffered.

Grollman, Earl, ed.   *Bereaved Children and Teens.* Boston: Beacon Press, 1995.

Rabbi Grollman has published many helpful books on grief work with children. This one is valuable because is offers essays by pastoral experts in many different Christian traditions as well as Jewish tradition. There are essays that address the interests of young children and also adolescents. You can find help to prepare a child for an imminent death as well as to follow up in days, weeks and even years following a death.

Inbody, Tyron

The Transforming God. Louisville, KY: Westminster/John Knox Press, 1997.

The author used this material to help college students look at the various ways Christian tradition has interpreted suffering over the centuries. He works towards his own model of understanding who God is for us and with us in the midst of tragic circumstances. It is not easy to read but my students in theological college appreciated it deeply. Sometimes a way of thinking about God makes suffering worse; this book offers many approaches to God when we confront life's most painful questions.

Lester, Andrew, ed.

When Children Suffer: A Sourcebook for Ministry with Children in Crisis. Philadelphia: Westminster Press, 1987.

This series of essays draws on the authors' wealth of denominational backgrounds and pastoral experience, and contains careful discussion of issues for children of different ages facing similar kinds of suffering. The collection goes beyond encounters with death to consider the ways children suffer when facing divorce, chronic illness, hospitalization, abuse, disability and anxiety. Most essays enrich an adult's understanding of how children suffer, but there are concrete examples of approaches to try with children in some of the essays.

Nouwen, Henri.   *The Wounded Healer.* New York:
                     Doubleday, 1972.

A classic by a great Christian teacher, this book helps us
consider that the wounds we have experienced in our lives do
not prevent us from caring for others with compassion and
strength. My students have often found this book confronts
them with their own desire to respond perfectly to others. Such
perfection is beyond us, Nouwen confesses, but God's healing
grace still works through us. This perspective is very important
to consider for adults working with children!

Suchocki, Marjorie   *The Fall to Violence: Original Sin in Rela-
                      tional Theology.* New York: Continuum,
                      1994.

This author considers some of the most distressing situations we confront in the world. From the violence of war to
the brutality of street crime, she considers where we can find
God in the face of terrifying events. Her understanding of the
situation of victims is profound as she struggles to consider
what Jesus' command to forgive means when violence has oc-
curred. Her wrestling with a new meaning for "original sin"
can prepare us for the hardest questions anyone can ask!

Weems, Ann   *Psalms of Lament.* Louisville, KY:
                      Westminster/John Knox Press, 1995.

Weems is known in North America for her collections of
poetry reflecting on gospel stories. This collection is a moving
testimony to the depth of her faith. She speaks in the introduc-

tion about the death of her son and her own struggle to find God again from the depths of her grief. Her psalms agonize with God in the tradition of biblical psalms. It is not an easy collection to read, and yet its cry to the depths of sorrow and anger that accompany tragic loss rings true.

Young, Frances   *Face to Face: A Narrative Essay in the Theology of Suffering.* Edinburgh: T&T Clark, 1990.

The narrator is both a theologian and a mother who reflects on her life with her severely handicapped son. Her story grapples with her own emotions, the challenges her whole family faces, and her questions about God – and to God. She teaches much about the themes of suffering in Christian tradition as she faces her past assumptions, her present life and her family's future. She doesn't shy away from any issue.

Pursuing Adults' Questions about Faith and Christian Tradition

Many people who have the opportunity to study Christian faith and tradition often discover that they thought they "had" to believe something that scholars and other believers debate quite openly. Such a discovery can be both liberating and frightening! My conviction is that God is always greater than our questions and more mysterious than the perspective we currently hold. I offer a few suggestions of books that students and colleagues recommended to me as "refreshing" and helpful. I don't agree with every author on every point, that's for sure, but these books are thought-provoking. Your own Church may also have published an introduction of the faith as it is formally taught in your tradition. Be sure to seek out such a resource, too.

Bass, Dorothy, ed.   *Practicing Our Faith: A Way of Life for a Searching People*. San Francisco: Jossey-Bass, 1997.

This collection of essays considers central themes in Christian discipleship from contemporary perspectives. Authors come from a variety of Christian and social backgrounds. They help readers develop a fresh appreciation for traditional themes of the Christian life, emphasizing how we can live out our faith in significant ways every day. There are discussion questions at the end of each chapter for study groups to use.

Borg, Marcus   *Meeting Jesus Again for the First Time: The Historical Jesus & The Heart of Contemporary Faith*. New York: HarperSan Francisco, 1994.

Marcus Borg has become well known in the last decade for his ability to make current debates in New Testament scholarship accessible to those curious about issues in biblical interpretation. This book has helped many people who wondered if they were the only ones with questions about Jesus. Borg summarizes important issues and offers the reader a way to relate the New Testament witnesses to contemporary life.

Heschel, Abraham   *Man Is Not Alone: A Philosophy of Religion*. New York: The Noonday Press/Farrar, Straus & Giroux, 1959/1990.

Heschel's appreciation of wonder is presented in Chapter 2. His work offers a beautiful reflection on the presence of God in our lives and the experiences that provoke our amazement. He pulls us beyond any sense of faith as information about God to move more deeply into our encounters with God's mystery.

| Milton, Ralph | *Common Sense Christianity: The No-bafflegab Guide to the Christian Faith.* Winfield, BC/Ottawa: Wood Lake/Novalis, 1988. |

An easy-to-read ramble through the kinds of questions and objections contemporary people often raise to Christian faith. Milton is a storyteller who laces his teaching about tradition with amusing and thought-provoking anecdotes. The style is light-hearted but the questions addressed are profound – from science vs religion to God's relationship to people of many faiths.

| Norris, Kathleen | *Amazing Grace: A Vocabulary of Faith.* New York: Riverhead Books, 1998. |

Norris has combined her wonderful ability to tell stories with her reflections on a wide spectrum of Christian themes. She works through "angels" and "anger" to "worship" and "The New Jerusalem," drawing from her personal spiritual journey as well as the teachings of saints both ancient and contemporary. She has a marvellous way of opening up the healing power of ancient truth while confronting the arguments and ambiguities we face in contemporary life. Someone to whom I gave this book found it a gift of God's grace in a difficult time.

Ramshaw, Gail   *God Beyond Gender.* Minneapolis:
                                 Augsburg Fortress Press, 1995.

Here is an articulate presentation of issues raised in the debates about inclusive language. Ramshaw threads her way through important imagery from Scripture and tradition to help the reader understand its roots and its contemporary impact. She will not surrender the wisdom of Christian tradition, nor will she settle for language as it has "always" been used. Chances are English usage wasn't "always" the way we think!

Stairs, Jean   *Listening for the Soul: Pastoral Care and
                                 Spiritual Direction.* Minneapolis:
                                 Augsburg Fortress, 2000.

This book both encourages and instructs those who hope to nourish "soulfulness" in the lives of Christian people. Chapters work through a variety of life situations and sustaining spiritual practices, some from tradition and some with contemporary creativity. There is an important chapter on children's spirituality that, like other chapters, offers spiritual exercises and reflection questions at the end.

Suchocki, Marjorie   *In God's Presence: Theological Reflections on
                                 Prayer.* St. Louis, MO: Chalice Press,
                                 1996.

Insights from this book are shared in Chapter 3. The author works through the many kinds of prayers in Christian tradition, offering ways to think about how God engages us when we pray. My students found her ideas helpful when working on dilemmas that arise in a life of prayer.

Whitehead, Evelyn & James
Christian Life Patterns: The Psychological Challenges and Religious Invitations of Adult Life. New York: Crossroad, 1996.

Here is a companion for adults whose spiritual questions change as they mature. Drawing on the work of Erik Erikson, the Whiteheads combine psychological and spiritual insight into many common challenges and transitions that arise for adults in Western societies. Each chapter begins with a reflection and some questions to draw the reader's personal experience into conversation with the book's points of view.

The Work of Stories

In Chapter 1, I mentioned the resurgence of storytelling and the respect for the work of stories that has grown over the last 25 years. I hesitate to recommend titles in an area that stretches across so many disciplines and has many significant debates among theorists and practitioners. And yet my encounter with storytelling as an approach to preaching and pastoral care changed my life! So I offer a few titles from different disciplines with differing points of view because I found them interesting. A couple of these books I rely on as a pastor and teacher. The others provoke me to think and to read new things and to listen to stories with a keener ear.

Coles, Robert
The Call of Stories: Teaching and the Moral Imagination. Boston: Houghton Mifflin, 1989.

Coles' work is introduced in Chapter 1 through this important examination of his approach to teaching. As he reflects on the literature he has used with his students, he offers stories of their reactions and insights sure to stimulate the reader as well. Here is an invitation for all who love stories to deepen both understanding and respect for the power of storytelling in healing and transforming human lives.

Fulford, Robert *The Triumph of Narrative: Storytelling in the Age of Mass Culture.* Toronto: House of Anansi Press, 1999.

Fulford's 1999 Massey Lectures translate well as essays probing the place of storytelling in a world where stories are marketed in a variety of ways. His voice cautions us about the ways in which narrative can be co-opted by power interests and reminds us that discerning the truth in a story is a necessary and complex feature of contemporary life.

Groome, Thomas *Sharing Faith: A Comprehensive Approach to Religious Education and Pastoral Ministry.* San Francisco: HarperSanFrancisco, 1991.

Groome is a professor of religious education whose groundbreaking work on *praxis* changed my approach to ministry twenty years ago. This book is not for the faint-hearted because it examines in detail important philosophical debates about human knowing and their influence in Christian tradition. For those schooled in the practice of ministry or teaching, it provides an in-depth source and model for the work of storytelling in religious education and in pastoral care.

McAdams, Dan   *The Stories We Live By: Personal Myths and the Making of the Self.* New York: The Guilford Press, 1993.

One of my favourite books, this work offers insight into the place of stories as people move through life. McAdams' work with children shapes my analysis in Chapter 1. His insights into adolescence and his model inviting adults to tell their life stories are both exceptionally valuable. You can learn more about yourself and the formative events in your life in conversation with McAdams' research.

Nussbaum, Martha   *Poetic Justice: The Literary Imagination and Public Life.* Boston: Beacon Press, 1995.

Nussbaum's interest in the ethical values implicit in public policy debates makes this a fascinating book. She demonstrates how characters in fiction draw out our values and challenge us to think about the implications of policies we support. I have used her approach in the classroom, choosing fiction that portrays different perspectives on faith and values. Students suddenly recognize arguments from textbooks taking flesh in the interaction of characters.

Quindlen, Anna   *How Reading Changed My Life.* New York: Library of Contemporary Thought, 1998.

Quindlen's engaging reminiscence of her life as a reader and lover of books draws other readers to recall those books that left an impact over the years. A gifted storyteller and columnist, this author helps us treasure the pleasures of books in an age when some have pronounced them obsolete. Her lists of books – to recommend to teenagers, to take on summer holiday, to save in a fire, etc. – provide worthy suggestions for further reading and also inspire reflection on what we would put on our own lists.

Shea, John   *Stories of God: An Unauthorized Biography.* Chicago: St. Thomas More Press, 1978.

In the earliest days of "narrative theology," John Shea emerged as an influential and creative interpreter as well as a delightful storyteller. This book could also appear in the category "Pursuing Adults' Faith Questions" because Shea deftly translates the weighty language of Christian tradition into the accessible world of storytelling. He presses important theological questions by bringing the stories of Scripture into conversation with the experience and questions of contemporary believers.

Taylor, Daniel   *The Healing Power of Stories: Creating Yourself Through the Stories of Your Life.* New York: Doubleday, 1996.

Taylor combines his knowledge of English literature with his ability to tell stories in a framework that invites adults to reconsider their life stories. He probes difficult areas in human experience with the conviction that broken stories can be healed. His work can help adults address their own childhood stories so that they can listen clearly to the stories today's children have to tell.

White, Michael
& Epston, David

Narrative Means to Therapeutic Ends. New York: Norton, 1990.

This classic textbook introduces what is now known as "narrative therapy" in the words and case studies of the founders of this approach. While reading a book on therapy never turns the reader into a practitioner, I found this book helped me listen to children in new ways. Many cases that are reported present quite young people with problems to discuss. A narrative therapy approach to problem solving respects a child's way of thinking about themselves and working with the world.

Notes

1   Robert Coles, *The Call of Stories: Teaching and the Moral Imagination.* Boston: Houghton Mifflin, 1989.

2   Martha Nussbaum, *Poetic Justice: The Literary Imagination and Public Life.* Boston: Beacon Press, 1995.

3   Robert Coles, *The Spiritual Life of Children* (Boston: Houghton Mifflin, 1990).

4   James Fowler, *Stages of Faith: The Psychology of Human Development and the Quest for Meaning* (New York: Harper & Row, 1981), 149.

5   Dan McAdams, *The Stories We Live By: Personal Myths and the Making of the Self* (New York: The Guilford Press, 1993), 67-68.

6   Ibid., 71.

7   Robert Coles, *The Moral Intelligence of Children.* (New York: Random House, 1997), 29.

8   Abraham Heschel, *Man Is Not Alone: A Philosophy of Religion* (New York: The Noonday Press/ Farrar, Straus & Giroux, 1951/1990), 12, 68.

9   Ibid., 37.

10 Robert Coles, *The Spiritual Life of Children.* See the unpaginated section of children's art in the middle of the book.

11 John Hull, *God-talk with Young Children* (Philadelphia: Trinity Press International, 1991).

12 Marjorie Suchocki, *In God's Presence* (St. Louis, MO: Chalice Press, 1996), 50.

13 Sonja Stewart and Jerome Berryman, *Young Children and Worship* (Louisville, KY: Westminster/John Knox Press, 1989).

14 Herbert Anderson & Susan Johnson, *Regarding Children: A New Respect for Childhood and Families* (Louisville, KY: Westminster/John Knox Press, 1994).

Meet Fergie the Frog!

Stories by Nancy L. Cocks
Illustrations by Jirina Marton

Fergie Tries to Fly
Frogs may not be able to fly, but they have other talents, as Fergie discovers when a baby bird falls into the pond.

Where Oh Where Is Fergie?
When two children frognap Fergie, will he ever find a way to return to the swamp?

You Can Count on Fergie
Fergie may not be the best at math, but when it comes to being a good friend, he gets top marks.

Nobody Loves Fergie

Fergie's big brother, Freddie, seems to be getting all the attention these days. Doesn't anybody love Fergie anymore?

Fergie Cleans Up

The swamp is a mess when human campers come to stay for a few days. How can they be so thoughtless?

Fergie Counts His Blessings

When Fergie misses Frog Scout camp because of math homework, he decides to run away and start a new life on his own.

Fergie Has a Birthday Party

Fergie needs one more guest for his party, but how can he invite a toad? Everyone knows frogs and toads don't mix!

Fergie Goes to Grandma's

Fergie would rather hunt gnats than go to Grandma's, but when he spends an afternoon listening to Grandma's adventures he realizes she's pretty special after all.

Wild Goose Publications is part of

The Iona Community

The Iona Community, founded in 1938 by the Revd George MacLeod, then a parish minister in Glasgow, is an ecumenical Christian community committed to seeking new ways of living the Gospel in today's world. Initially working to restore part of the medieval abbey on Iona, the Community today remains committed to 'rebuilding the common life' through working for social and political change, striving for the renewal of the church with an ecumenical emphasis, and exploring new, more inclusive approaches to worship, all based on an integrated understanding of spirituality.

The Community now has over 240 Members, about 1500 Associate Members and around 1500 Friends. The Members – women and men from many denominations and backgrounds (lay and ordained), living throughout Britain with a few overseas – are committed to a fivefold Rule of devotional discipline, sharing and accounting for use of time and money, regular meeting, and action for justice and peace.

At the Community's three residential centres – the Abbey and the MacLeod Centre on Iona, and Camas Adventure Camp on the Ross of Mull – guests are welcomed from March to October and over Christmas. Hospitality is provided for over 110 people, along with a unique opportunity, usually through week-long programmes, to extend horizons and forge relationships through sharing an experience of the common life in worship, work, discussion and relaxation. The Community's shop on Iona, just outside the Abbey grounds, carries an attractive range of books and craft goods.

The Community's administrative headquarters are in Glasgow, which also serves as a base for its work with young people, the Wild Goose Resource Group working in the field of worship, a bi-monthly magazine, *Coracle*, and a publishing house, Wild Goose Publications.

For information on the Iona Community contact:
The Iona Community, Fourth Floor, Savoy House, 140 Sauchiehall Street,
Glasgow G2 3DH, UK. Phone: 0141 332 6343
e-mail: ionacomm@gla.iona.org.uk; web: www.iona.org.uk

For enquiries about visiting Iona, please contact:
Iona Abbey, Isle of Iona, Argyll PA76 6SN, UK. Phone: 01681 700404
e-mail: ionacomm@iona.org.uk

Wild Goose Publications, the publishing house of the Iona Community established in the Celtic Christian tradition of St Columba, produces books, tapes and CDs on:

- holistic spirituality
- social justice
- political and peace issues
- healing
- innovative approaches to worship
- song in worship, including the work of the Wild Goose Resource Group
- material for meditation and reflection

If you would like to find out more about our books, tapes and CDs, please contact us at:

Wild Goose Publications
Fourth Floor, Savoy House
140 Sauchiehall Street,
Glasgow G2 3DH, UK

Tel. +44 (0)141 332 6292
Fax +44 (0)141 332 1090
e-mail: admin@ionabooks.com

or visit our website at
www.ionabooks.com
for details of all our products and online sales